PLANTING BY THE MOON

1999

PLANTING
BY THE
MOON

A GARDENERS' CALENDAR

1999

Nick Kollerstrom

PROSPECT BOOKS

Published in 1998 by Prospect Books,
Allaleigh House, Blackawton, Totnes, Devon TQ9 7DL, England.

British Library Cataloguing in Publication Data:
A catalogue entry of this book is available from the British Library.

Typeset by Tom Jaine.
Layout, illustrations and figures by Philippa Stockley.
Cover design by Philippa Stockley.

Printed by the Cromwell Press, Trowbridge, Wiltshire.

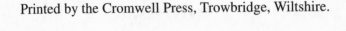

CONTENTS

FIGURES

INTRODUCTION

> To everything there is a season and a time to every purpose under heaven: a time
> to be born and time to die: a time to plant, and a time to pluck up what is planted.
>
> *Ecclesiastes,* 3:1-2

HAVE YOU EVER WONDERED whether your garden vegetables would benefit if you planted them in synchrony with the phases and the cycles of the Moon?

Since time immemorial, man has held a belief in the efficacy of such a practice in various guises and according to different traditions which have developed on this subject. In many countries today lunar calendars are available for farmers and gardeners. There is now considerable evidence that crops can benefit from the right use of a lunar gardening guide, as this 1999 issue of *Planting by the Moon* attempts to show.

It must be said, however, that present-day lunar gardening guides do disagree with each other on just about every recommendation they make. Old traditions on the subject have grown confused with the passage of time and a new start has appeared within the twentieth-century organic farming/gardening movement known as Bio-Dynamics. The guide you are now reading differs from others in that it spends a few chapters reviewing the subject as a whole, before coming out with its own calendar structure. Folk-traditions are described, as also is the evidence of modern studies. The book is for readers who want a practical grower's guide to the cycles of time and for those who would like to develop more of a perspective on the issues involved.

The aim is to stimulate interest and research in the area as well as to improve your vegetables. The reader is introduced to various modern studies concerned with the question of lunar influence, placed within the context of the burgeoning organic movement. But those who simply wish to apply the recommended sowing times for 1999 can turn straight to those chapters that talk about how to use the calendar itself. These recommendations are not the same as those in other lunar gardening guides but they may have a better chance of producing dependable crop improvements.

A gardener works with time. He or she has continually to make judgements of how the seasons are progressing, what the weather may do, and so forth, while simultaneously considering the limited time available. Gardening and farming take on an extra dimension if one is aware that, besides these mundane considerations, there are also basic cycles of the heavens to which animals and the plant world are very much attuned. Plants receive their energy for growth from the sun but, in other more subtle ways, they are continually affected by the Moon's ever-changing rhythms. A decision as to when to plant a tree should take such lunar cycles into account, just as a sailor puts to sea only when the tides are right.

With my colleague Simon Best, I produced earlier versions of *Planting by the Moon* in the 1980s. This new edition is concerned to reaffirm our advice, but has several new features in addition. It has, for example, data from years of racehorse breeding which has not hitherto been published. The book is intended as a 'hardy annual' and future editions may not contain the critique of different schools of thought as is here presented. A more detailed work describing the evidence on which it is based is planned shortly. My collaborator Simon Best has been busy elsewhere but may return as co-author in the future as much has developed from our original synthesis.

The idea that the Moon exerts a determinable influence on plant and crop growth may be as old as agriculture. The idea is found embedded in the folklore of many ancient societies, ranging from the Celts in early Britain to the Maoris in New Zealand. As far as recorded comments on the subject are concerned, Pliny the Elder (AD 23–79), the Roman historian, in his *Natural History*[72] gives many instructions on how to regulate agricultural activities according to the cycles of the Moon.

With the dawn of modern science the Moon was reduced to a lifeless orb which influenced nothing but the tides and marine creatures. Beliefs which until then had been taken for granted, that astronomical factors and the changing Moon were important for the growth of crops, became discredited and lingered on only as superstition and old wives' tales. So it remained until relatively recently.

During the twentieth century, systematic experiments began to determine how the various lunar cycles played a part in plant metabolism, growth and development. Certain keys to understanding the relationship of plant response to lunar influence have now emerged and can be incorporated into a gardener's or farmer's plans as to when best to carry out various tasks, in particular sowing, planting* and harvesting.

This manual is presented more as an invitation to gardeners and others to investigate the time cycles involved in plant growth than as a dogmatic statement of how they work. It is an attempt at a synthesis of time-honoured traditions and twentieth-century research. Except where stated, all the advice and knowledge is based on experimentation. This is cited, with explanatory graphs and diagrams where appropriate. Although we are responsible for all the statements that appear in this manual, we would like to acknowledge the influence of the work of the two women, Lili Kolisko (1889–1976) and Maria

---

*Here and throughout the term 'planting' includes the sowing of seed as well as the planting of seedlings.

Thun (*b*. 1922), on our own research and conclusions. While differing from them on some fundamental issues, we nevertheless recognize them as pioneers in lunar-planting research.

There are various astrological and related concepts used in the calendar. Readers unfamiliar with such things need not worry however. Clear step-by-step explanations are given in separate chapters. A star-calendar useful for gardeners is here presented, composed of two kinds of process: on the one hand there are rhythms of energy that pulse, or ebb and flow, in approximately nine-day cycles which should resonate with the sympathetic worker; and there are specific moments, celestial events, which the gardener should endeavour to catch.

It is our hope that this manual will come to be used not only for its practical advantages but also as an inspiration to gardeners to become more aware of the life-rhythms in nature which mysteriously connect the growth of plants with cosmic time-cycles.

Chapter 1

PERSPECTIVES

Pleiades rising in the dawning sky,
    Harvest is nigh.
Pleiades setting in the waning night,
    Ploughing is right.
Forty days and nights in the turning year
    They disappear.
When they shine again in the morning shade,
    Sharpen your blade.

Hesiod, *Works and Days* (Eighth century BC)

PLANTS ARE ADAPTED to the primary cycles of time – the day, the month and the year. This book focuses on the second of these, on the monthly rhythms which are so important for the plant world. These monthly cycles are lunar, in contrast with the day and the year which are solar. It may be a mystery as to how plants respond to these monthly cycles, but that doesn't stop them from being of practical value in farm and garden.

The sensitivity of plants to minute levels of energy was first systematically studied by the Indian scientist Sir Jagadis Chandra Bose (1858–1937) in the early years of this century.[13] Using carefully designed apparatus, he produced a mass of evidence showing that plants have a far greater capacity to respond to subtle environmental stimuli than had previously been believed.

Plants, small animals and birds seem to be attuned to the natural electric and magnetic fields of the Earth. By altering such fields in a laboratory, scientists have been able to alter the rate and other characteristics of a plant's growth, and the direction in which a bird will fly. Earth's geomagnetic field has a large lunar-monthly component to its variation.

The Biosphere

One of the first lunar-cycle effects to be clearly demonstrated was in rainfall. This was reported in 1962, by two independent groups of researchers, one in the northern and one in the southern hemisphere. Their results appeared in *Science* magazine – in the same issue, for mutual support![14] The Moon pulls on the sea according to a twice-monthly rhythm, so that tides reach their highest twice a month, every 14.7 days. Likewise, the amount of rainfall on average also shows a twice-monthly cycle, peaking three or four days after the Full and New positions. The highest tides, for comparison, appear on average a day after the Full and New positions, they have a lag of one day. The two groups of researchers examined a good half-century of data, and found that the magnitude of the lunar effect they had discovered depended on the level of solar activity.

The Earth is surrounded by a large magnetic field, which acts like a membrane which protects us from solar radiation. This pulsates to a monthly rhythm, becoming strongest on the days following the Full Moon – as was again discovered by another two independent US groups.[7,82] The GMF (geomagnetic field) stays low for the week prior to the Full Moon, then it increases sharply, remaining high for some days afterwards.

Thunderstorms recorded by eastern US weather stations over the years 1942–1965 showed a peak two days after the Full Moon,[61] just as did the geomagnetism data. They decreased for a few days before the Full Moon, followed by a sharp increase. Conversely, there was a definite decrease on days following the New Moon. In contrast, a survey of hurricanes and typhoons in the North Atlantic, from 80 years of data, found they tended to occur twenty per cent more frequently on days following both the Full and New Moons.[21]

So, the biosphere as a whole responds to this fundamental cycle, either in a monthly or a fortnightly rhythm. The effect of this pulsation upon climate is science, not just folklore. The changing Sun-Moon angle causes huge electric and magnetic changes in the upper atmosphere. It is therefore little more than common sense to affirm that a farmer should take notice of it.

Traditional Lore

There is a wide but fragmentary body of folk-knowledge, gleaned from many cultures and various ages, that reflects the age-old belief of farmers and gardeners that the Moon somehow influences the growth of their crops. Hesiod, the Greek astronomer and contemporary of Homer, is considered to have written the first lunar agricultural manual, in the eighth century BC. His poem *Works and Days* advised farmers how to regulate many activities by the phases of the Moon.[43] Later, this emphasis on the lunar phases became particularly important to the Roman farmer. Lunar planting rules were recorded by such writers as Cato and Pliny.[83] The primary rules, many of which have persisted in folklore to this day, focus on the differences between the effects of the waxing and waning Moon.

Basically, whatever required growth or development was started during the waxing phase, and whatever needed to dry, cure or decrease without decay was dealt with in the waning. Just before New Moon, at the dark of the Moon, was said to be especially favourable for the latter activities. Thus, the planting of crops, picking of grapes for wine and shearing of sheep were carried out during the waxing Moon, and the general harvesting of crops, felling of timber and castration of animals during the waning phase.

Pliny was a keen observer of nature, shown by his multi-volume *History of Nature*. He believed he could discern how, 'that tiny creature the ant, at the moon's conjunction keeps quite quiet, but at full moon works busily even in the nights.'[72] If there was a problem with the ground being damp, then Pliny's advice was to sow seeds in the waning half of the lunar cycle so that it might dry out. Seventeenth-century British gardening guides quoted Pliny in this regard.[44]

The various facets of lunar lore were transmitted, both verbally and in scattered writings, down through the ages and across cultures to the present, although modern collections of these adages illustrate markedly the confusion of ideas in this area.[5] Grafting and planting-out operations should be performed during the waxing Moon, because rising sap is said to aid the formation of new shoots or the establishment of a new graft. Lawns are said to benefit from being sown during the waxing phase, a time also propitious for the transplanting of trees and flowers. One of the oldest maxims using the waxing/waning division with respect to planting is as follows: crops which produce their yield above ground should be planted during the waxing Moon, whereas those that produce below ground should be sown during the waning Moon. This idea can be found in many parts of the world, but so can similar ideas which modify or contradict it.

In particular, it is claimed that sowing around the Full or New Moon will improve crop growth. Here again opinions vary: for example, some advocate planting in the days immediately preceding the New Moon so that seeds will have germinated and be ready to grow as the Moon begins to increase. More widespread is the opposite opinion, that crops should be sown just before the Full Moon, the view particularly associated with the work of Lili Kolisko. She came to Britain from Germany in 1936, and the results of her years of study were published in 1938–9[51,52] claiming that seed germination, and especially the unfolding of the first leaves of young shoots, pointed to the days prior to Full Moon as an optimal sowing-time, while those prior to New Moon were the worst, or rather slowest, in growth.

However, as will be discussed in Chapter 4, although Moon phase does affect plant metabolism, there is little reliable evidence that sowing at any particular point in the lunar-phase cycle will influence the final yield. Seedling germination and growth may increase around and especially just before the Full Moon, but such effects may not show up in the final crop yield. Much of the confusion of traditional beliefs may have arisen from such a confounding of different aspects of plant growth.

That crops should be harvested according to the phase of the Moon was widely accepted by farmers of antiquity. Pliny the Elder described the then customary practice of harvesting crops needed for storage near the New Moon, when they would be driest and preserve the best, or gathering those that were to be eaten fresh at Full Moon:

> for it makes a very great difference whether one wants to store the crop or put it
> on the market, because grain increases in bulk when the Moon is waxing.

The very same view was current in seventeenth-century England:

> he [the farmer] shall gather and carry into his house whatsoever he would have
> to endure and last long, at such times as the Moone shall decrease.[35]

In more recent times, it used to be a common custom in the west of England to gather in the 'hoard fruit' in the shrinking of the Moon. Apples bruised in the harvesting would then tend to preserve better over the winter. This accords with modern studies showing varying plant water-absorption at the different phases, suggesting that some facets of lunar lore may be vindicated by modern research.

The Four Elements

At the present time, a variety of lunar gardening guides is available but, alas, they disagree over just about every recommendation they give. Despite this, there would seem to be one thing which they have in common: they all use some notion of the fourfold division of the zodiac into periods that each influence a particular element (earth, air, fire and water). This means that they all have a nine-day rhythm for sowing crops – let's explain that.

The scheme here used has developed within the context of Bio-Dynamic farming, which has the longest tradition of organic gardening in the twentieth century.[30] It was founded in 1924 by the Austrian teacher and philosopher Rudolf Steiner (1861–1925), the founder of the Anthroposophist movement. It attempts to use holistic principles, viewing the farm as an integral whole and taking account of the condition of the cosmos.[77]

At the core of the Bio Dynamic calendar is a four-element pattern, generated by the motion of the Moon against the stars. Each month, the Moon moves around the sky against the twelve constellations of the zodiac. This means that every two or three days it enters a new constellation, each of which has its particular affinity with one of the four elements.

The elements are Earth, Water, Air and Fire and these are deemed to influence the growth and performance of a particular sort of plant, respectively root, leaf, flower and fruit or seed. This model is specifically a four-element theory, in which the further division into the twelve signs of the zodiac is very

EARTH ELEMENT: ROOT

Taurus   *Virgo*   *Capricorn*

WATER ELEMENT: LEAF

Cancer   *Scorpio*   *Pisces*

AIR ELEMENT: FLOWER

Gemini   *Libra*   *Aquarius*

FIRE ELEMENT: FRUIT OR SEED

Aries   *Leo*   *Sagittarius*

much secondary. It is a modern application of a very ancient idea, that of the four elements. There are parallels in the discovery by scientists that there are twelve types of 'fundamental' particles, or in the description by biochemists of four types of code in the DNA strand, or in physicists' four states of matter – solid, liquid, gas and plasma (hot, and above the atmosphere) – just as Jungian psychology has four temperaments. So this elemental theory underpinning our understanding of plant growth uses four types of 'formative force'. These form-forces link time of sowing to the final condition of the crop when it is harvested.

For readers new to the idea, let's just say: first one builds a house, establishing the foundations and structure – Earth. Then one fits in the water supply (Water). Next one checks out that it will be adequately ventilated (Air) and lastly one fits in the heating and electricity (Fire). It's quite natural: in fact, it's elementary.

The ancient Greeks applied the theory in their four temperaments, much used in their medical practice. The melancholic was pensive and prone to depression (Earth), while a choleric character was impulsive and fiery and of thin and wiry build. A phlegmatic character (Water) was emotionally sensitive but prone to becoming overweight.

The four-element theory was first expressed by Empedocles in the fifth century BC in Sicily (shortly before he jumped into Mount Etna). Mother Nature used the four elements to paint with, he explained, in a long poem, just as an artist uses four colours. He didn't say what the four colours were! In fire and wind, in sea and

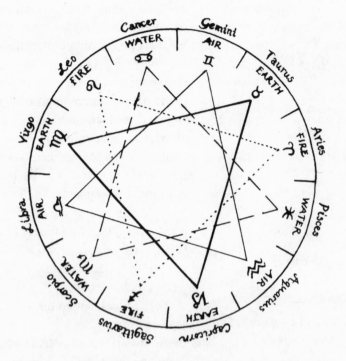

Figure 1. The four-element cycle underlying the zodiac.

stone, Empedocles discerned this fourfold pattern. He would surely have appreciated the new twist to his theory in the twentieth century.

What are here called root-days are the times to sow carrots, potatoes and the like. These days occur, for example, when the Moon passes in front of the stars of Taurus, the Bull, when the Moon is said to be 'in' Taurus. Taurus is viewed as having an 'earth' type of energy, and this earth-type of energy is linked with sowing root-crops – hence, 'root-days'. So, the root-days have an astronomical definition, and are timed by the Moon's motion against the stars.

There are three constellations linked to the Earth element, spaced equally around the circle of the zodiac. Taurus, we have mentioned. The other two are Virgo (the Virgin) and Capricorn (the Goat). Because it takes 27 days for the Moon to go once round (as will be explained in the next chapter), one set of root-days for planting potatoes will turn up every nine days. The diagram shows the sky-triangle that maps the three Earth-signs.

Lettuce or broccoli are sown or planted on leaf-days, these being times when the Moon is in front of the constellations that have traditionally been viewed as 'watery'. The three water constellations of the zodiac are Pisces (the Fish), Cancer (the Crab) and Scorpio (the Scorpion). In exactly the same manner as the constellations that are reckoned to influence the earth element, they form a triangle in the sky. Thus, the 27-day orbit of the moon against the stars produces three periods of the same element. So, if the weather is unsuitable for sowing lettuce, one just waits for the next set of 'leaf-days', nine days later. Flower-days (Air) and fruit-seed days (Fire, or Warmth) complete the picture.

Calendars based upon this four-element structure have been published and acted upon for more than 30 years. Their utility and accuracy are beginning to acquire a time-tested quality. Some reports of long-term trials are described below.

In using this model, our calendar assumes that there are four types of crop:

Root-days
Element: EARTH
Example of crop: carrot, radish, potato
Moon-constellation: Taurus, Virgo, Capricorn

Leaf-days
Element: WATER
Example of crop: lettuce, cabbage
Moon-constellation: Scorpio, Cancer, Pisces

Flower-days
Element: AIR
Example of crop: cauliflower, globe artichoke, broccoli
Moon-constellation: Gemini, Libra, Aquarius

Fruit/seed-days
Element: FIRE
Example of crop: tomato, peas, beans
Moon-constellation: Leo, Aries, Sagittarius

One can visualize this as a sequence of plant development: first the root descends into the soil (Earth), then the leaves unfold, with water flowing up the stem and transpiring out through the leaves (Water). Then come the flowers, emitting their fragrance to attract bees and butterflies to fertilize them (Air). Lastly, the flowers fall away as the heat of the summer shrivels up the plant, drying it into the final stage of the seed (Fire). The tiny seeds contain the essence of the flower, just as fire is the least material or least dense of the four elements. Biologically, one may prefer to view the last stage as Warmth rather than Fire, emphasizing its constructive role in a process of maturation.

As a sequence in time, this goes root-days, flower-days, leaf-days and then fruit/seed-days. This repeats every nine days. The calendar is concerned with the zodiac in terms of this 'elementary' division according to the four elements.

The theory is that in nature there are four kinds of subtle-energy 'formative forces', which work to influence the way a plant will develop, and that these are activated by the Moon's passage through the zodiac-elements, as the seed is sown. This pattern of influence is to do with the stars, the real stars, and not with the zodiac used in modern sun-sign astrology. This is a difficult issue, and readers who wish to grapple with it may do so in Chapter 5.

Using a star-rhythm in a calendar sounds OK, one may say, but does it work? Chapter 4 looks at the evidence but, for now, let's just note that in 1979 the result of eight years of sowing experiments appeared, co-authored by Maria Thun (pronounced 'Toon'), who pioneered the theory back in 1956,[89] and statistician Dr Hans Heinze.[90] Each year, they had sown twelve rows of potatoes per lunar month, and then compared their final yields. These trials showed a zodiac rhythm in weight-yield per row that was highly significant. All of the debate and all of the evidence concerns this very physical thing, the final weight-yield of rows of vegetables. The distant stars are supposed to be doing this, which some readers may find credulity-straining. I did.

Such crop-yield experiments use twelve, or even twenty-four or thirty-six, rows of a given type of vegetable, each grown for the same length of time. It was always a surprise that it was the zodiac rhythm and not a moon-phase effect which showed up in the final yields.[56] That is hardly what traditional lore would predict. But organic growers are concerned with quality rather than mere quantity, and the biggest vegetables may not be the tastiest, so we will also be looking at 'quality' in this context.

This element-cycle (whose framework is 'sidereal' – see next chapter) is one of the two fundamental lunar cycles relevant for a lunar-gardening calendar. The other is the better-known waxing-waning lunar month of 29.5 days, which influences fertility, germination, water absorption and metabolism.[42] (NB, there does not exist any 28-day lunar cycle, contrary to widespread belief.) Chapter 3 looks at the evidence for this primary cycle affecting living things and why a modern grower should take notice of it. The sidereal rhythm is especially relevant to organic gardening. There are indications that it requires a decent 'living' soil for the element-rhythm to work; whereas, in contrast, lunar-phase effects will turn up anywhere!

Belief in the Moon's influence on the fertility of plants was once firmly embedded in the consciousness of ancient peoples. As science comes again to discover these subtle links between earth and sky farmers may again regard the application of lunar cycles as a sensible and valuable practice.

Chapter 2

CYCLES OF THE SKY

Time faire, to sowe or to gather be bold,
> but set or remoove when the weather is cold.
Cut all thing or gather, the Moone in the wane,
> but sowe in encreasing, or give it his bane.

Thomas Tusser, *Five Hundred Points of Good Husbandry* (1573)

As WE LOOK AT the stars scattered across the night sky, and the ever-changing visage of the silvery Moon, we cannot but be struck by a sense of the primal mystery of the Cosmos. Are we linked to it in some fundamental way, or is that only wishful thinking? What of the ancient doctrine, 'as above, so below'? Why does that Moon always face us, and why is it the same apparent size as the Sun? How did it get into that nearly circular path so far away from us, far too large to be a proper satellite of Earth, more like a companion planet?

The Moon's motion can be expressed in terms of four main, monthly cycles. These describe its motion in relation to the Sun (synodic), to the stars (sidereal), to the Earth (apogee-perigee) and to the ecliptic plane (nodal). Let's look at them one by one.

The Synodic or Phase Cycle (Moon-Sun)

As the Moon waxes and wanes each month, it mirrors the Sun's light from different angles – the best known lunar cycle. It takes twenty-nine and a half

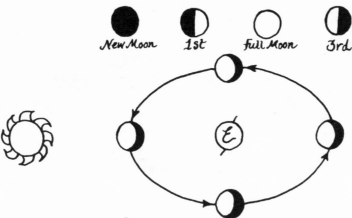

Figure 2. The synodic or phase cycle.

days to do this. When Full, the Moon is opposite to the Sun in the sky, so that as it rises, the Sun sets. The four positions of the Full, New and quarter-moons each month are shown in the calendar.

There are usually twelve Full Moons in a year. The months were originally lunar, and still are in the Jewish and Muslim calendars. To keep them in step with the solar year, a thirteenth month was added in every third year. This is called, intercalation. Muslims don't do this, so their twelve lunar months move round, with respect to the seasons, by eleven or so days every year.

Our two luminaries meet together in the sky at New Moon, when it becomes impossible to see the Moon for several days, because it is close to the Sun. The Greek word *synodos* means meeting. Let us note that this word also signified copulation, pointing to the deep connection this cycle has to germination and fertility. The next chapter will discuss this matter.

The Sidereal Cycle (Moon-Star)

Once in 27.3 days the Moon orbits around the Earth against the fixed stars. In this time, called a sidereal month (from the Latin, *sidera*, star) it returns to the same part of the heavens as seen from Earth. It also revolves on its own axis in this same period, enabling it to keep facing the Earth.

The Moon moves against the same background of star-constellations as do the other planets. It orbits around the Earth in a plane fairly similar to that in which the Earth and planets orbit around the Sun (called the Ecliptic). These constellations against which the Moon and planets are seen to move are therefore of special importance. Since ancient times they have been regarded

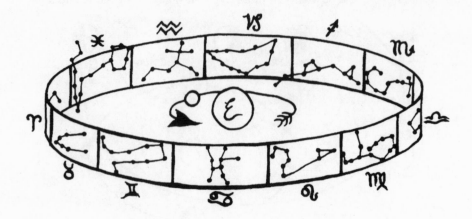

Figure 3. The sidereal cycle.

as divided into twelve, the twelve constellations of the zodiac. The Moon thus spends two to three days in each zodiacal constellation.

Chapter 4 describes how this cycle works in agriculture, then Chapter 5 looks at it from a different viewpoint, that of the 'sidereal' zodiac on which this calendar is based. This cycle has a special link with the four elements described earlier, as these colour the signs of the sidereal zodiac. Sky-triangles are thereby formed, and there is a handy German word, 'trigon,' by which Bio-Dynamic users refer to the three periods in a 'sidereal' month which influence the same element, for example the three sets of leaf-days.

The Apogee-Perigee Cycle (Moon-Earth)

The Moon moves around the Earth in an elliptical orbit, which means its distance from the Earth varies considerably through the month. Every 27.2 days it reaches its apogee, furthest away from the Earth, then at its perigee draws closest. At perigee it appears larger in the sky, pulls on the tides more strongly, and moves faster against the stars. This causes the time which the Moon spends in each of the twelve zodiacal divisions to vary by more than 30 per cent in a single rotation. At perigee, the Moon is moving fastest and it takes only two days to pass through one zodiacal division, whereas at apogee, when moving slowest, it takes almost three.

This cycle cannot be seen in the sky, as the change in size of the Moon's visage is too small to notice. Its effect can be seen in the calendar, however, whereby the Moon spends the least time moving through a sign at perigee, and the longest at apogee.

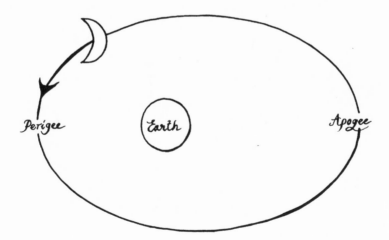

Figure 4. The apogee-perigee cycle.

The Nodal Cycle (Moon-Ecliptic)

The planets revolve around the Sun in approximately the same plane, the ecliptic, and the Moon's orbit is tilted at a slight angle, about five degrees, to this plane . This means that each month it rises above and then sinks below the Ecliptic. The two points at which it crosses the Ecliptic in each 27.5-day period are called nodes. When moving from south to north of the Ecliptic, the Moon reaches its north node and, when moving from north to south, its south node.

Eclipses can occur when the Moon reaches these points, and the ecliptic is so named because eclipses happen when Sun, Moon and Earth are in line and on this plane. When the Moon becomes New or Full close to a node, there will be, respectively, a solar or lunar eclipse. A solar eclipse draws a thin pencil of darkness upon the Earth, and its zone of totality' is confined to that line – such as will pass over the southern tip of Cornwall on August 11th 1999. A lunar eclipse, in contrast, is a reddish shadow that passes across the Moon, and is visible from one-half of the Earth.

The north and south nodes were called Dragon's Head and Dragon's Tail, respectively, indicating a belief that they were two special power points in the Moon's orbit – as if a menacing dragon were curled round the zodiac liable to swallow the Sun at some unpredictable moment.

A traditional British gardening guide advised readers to avoid sowing seeds 'over the dragon's tail' – the South Node – whereas the dragon's head was an acceptable time for these undertakings. This calendar, in common with Bio-Dynamic calendars, makes no distinction between the two lunar moments, advising avoidance of both of them at sowing time.

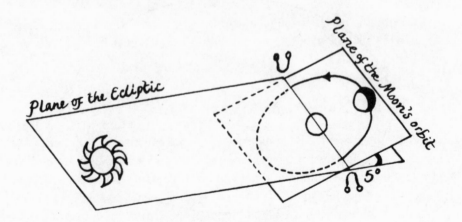

Figure 5. The nodal cycle.

The Moon 'Riding High'

The sidereal, monthly rhythm also expresses the varying height to which the Moon climbs above the horizon. On one day each month it arcs highest across the sky, and remains above the horizon for the longest time, then a fortnight later sinks to its least height above the horizon. American lunar-gardening manuals refer to these two halves of the month as 'riding high' and 'riding low.' The effect is very latitude-dependent, so in Scotland and northern countries one's experience of this cycle is more pronounced. There, the Moon hardly sets at one end of the month, then a fortnight later hardly rises.

Bio-Dynamic calendars allude to the two halves of this cycle as ascending, and descending. This reflects the Moon's monthly journey around the zodiac; the observed variation in its arc is due to the Earth's axis being tilted at an angle to the Ecliptic. It is the 27.3 day sidereal cycle viewed with reference to the Moon's height above the observer's horizon. The cycle gets confused with that of the waxing and waning Moon, and may account for similar recommendations to the above being ascribed to the waxing Moon period by English and American folklore.

This cycle mirrors the annual cycle of the Sun: in midwinter the Sun remains low above the horizon, and is then in front of the zodiac stars of Sagittarius, whereas in midsummer it rises high in the sky and is 'in' the constellation of Gemini. In midwinter, the Full Moon rises highest in the night sky, and it will then be 'in' the Gemini constellation, when the Sun, directly opposite, is in Sagittarius. Conversely, the midsummer Full Moon hangs very low above the horizon, in the constellation of Sagittarius. This cycle fades away near the Equator, then in the southern hemisphere is reversed, with both Sun and Moon rising highest against the stars of Sagittarius.

Bio-Dynamic calendars are characterized by their use of this cycle. They take the view that the planting-out of seedlings should be done in its 'descending' half.

The Harvest Moon

Each September a Full Moon appears, of special importance to farmers: the Harvest Moon. It rises for a week or so just around sunset, providing those extra few hours of illumination that can be so valuable at this time of year. Hanging large and low in the evening sky it often seems especially bright.

At the Autumnal equinox (about September 23rd) as the Sun crosses the equator into the southern hemisphere, the Ecliptic (the path of the Sun) is tilted at its lowest angle to the horizon. So the zodiac belt, containing the orbits of the Moon and planets, runs low above the horizon. For this astronomical reason, the Moon at this time rises only about 12 minutes later each day – whereas on average throughout the year it rises about 50 minutes later each day. Thus, at this time of harvesting, the Moon continues to rise soon after sunset for a number of successive evenings.

The Harvest Moon was held to be responsible for the ripening of produce, and, to the Romans, Diana's day fell at the time of the Harvest Full Moon, when offerings were made to her to ensure the ripening of their fruits. Seen through autumnal mists, the Moon often assumes a yellow hue. It then appears large in the sky due to its remaining close to the horizon, just as the Sun appears larger at sunset. The following Full Moon in October is called Hunter's Moon.

Use of a star-calendar has the advantage that it gives one a motivation for looking at the heavens. Anyone can recognize Orion and the Plough, but what about Taurus and Gemini? The ecliptic is that path through the constellations, along which the heavenly bodies move. In the afterglow of sunset, if the Moon and one or two planets are visible, one can trace its path as a line through the sky along which the Sun, Moon and planets all travel. Most of what is used in this calendar is visible to the naked eye in the sky above your garden.

Chapter 3

THE MOON AND FERTILITY

The thirteenth of the waxing month
Is a bad day to start seeding
But the best for transplanting.

Hesiod, *Works and Days.*

Figs, olives, apples, pears, vines can be planted at new moon, in the afternoon,
when there is no south wind.

Cato, *On Farming*

IN BRINGING TOGETHER this gardening guide, we take the view that modern
research gives sufficient basis to begin to sift the wheat from the chaff in these
old traditions. This is in itself a fairly new situation. For long it has appeared
that scientific belief and old lunar lore clashed completely, the former invali-
dating the latter.[7] But in recent decades a distinct change can be noted.[10]
Scientists are prepared to discuss how subtle changes in the Earth's magnetic
field are detected by organisms, investigate how birds use the lines of the
magnetic field for navigation and how they use certain star-constellations for
orientating themselves at night-time on their long migrations.[20] The germination of seeds has been found to depend upon the direction in which they are
aligned with respect to the magnetic field of the Earth. In this climate of
thought it no longer seems sheer moonshine to say that rhythms astronomical
in origin are important to a gardener.

'There seems little doubt that the lunar cycle influences the life processes
of plants,' wrote Dr Bernard Dixon, former editor of the *New Scientist.*[29] Dr
Dixon was referring to the Moon-phase cycle which affects many of the
growth-processes in a plant: its metabolic rate, absorption of water and
nutrients, rate of growth and its electrical activity have all been observed to
fluctuate in accordance with this rhythm.[18,54] This is of enormous significance
to farmers and gardeners.

The Phase Cycle and Plant Growth

The rate at which seeds germinate in relation to lunar phases was first studied
systematically in the 1930s by Kolisko, who concluded that wheat germinated
faster when sown at Full Moon than at New Moon.[51] Confirmation of this
result appeared in studies by M. Maw, funded by Canada's Department of
Agriculture, on the rate at which cress germinated. Over a six-month period,

batches of cress grown in water usually germinated quickest at Full Moon and slowest at New Moon, the difference in rate being very marked.[66]

Lunar-phase rhythms also appear in the rate at which plants grow, as was shown by Giorgio Abrami at the botanical gardens of Padua University.[3] Using several different species of herbaceous plants, taking a measure of their stem lengths every few days, he found, after applying a correction for daily temperature variations, that there were growth rhythms which, although different from one species to another, were phased according to Full and New Moon positions. Growth rates tended to be maximal at either the Full or New Moon positions.

Traditionally, it has always been assumed that sap in plants and trees rose most markedly during the Full Moon. Therefore, activities such as tree-felling should be performed at New Moon, and crops would preserve best if harvested at New Moon due to minimal water content. While direct evidence from studies of sap in trees and shrubs is scant, a study by Professor Frank Brown and Carol Chow investigated day-to-day variations in the absorption of water by bean seeds, under temperature-controlled conditions at their laboratory in North-western University, Illinois.[17] Each day, the amount of water the seeds absorbed over a four-hour period was measured. Large maxima were found to occur just before the Full Moon, absorption being on average 35 per cent higher than at New Moon.

Using wheat and pinto beans as her focus, a three-year study by Dr Jane Panzer, a biologist at Tulane University in the USA, confirmed the Brown and Chow findings regarding water absorption.[70] She found distinct lunar-related rhythms in water uptake, comparable to those Brown and his colleagues had

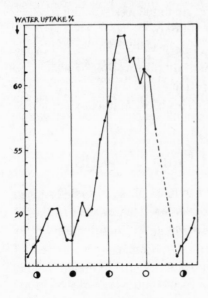

Figure 6. Water uptake by bean seeds (after Brown and Chow, 1973).

demonstrated, also a smaller effect observed with pinto beans which had been sterilized: The lunar link persisted, although to a lesser degree, even using pinto beans that had first been pasteurized or sterilized. She identified seasonal variations in this cycle of water uptake, as well as a rhythm in seed germination that mirrored the monthly patterns found for water absorption.

Biochemist Dr Harry Rounds at Wichita State University in the US reported that stress hormones in the blood of mice and men decreased sharply at Full and New Moon. He then extracted similar stress-related, 'cardio-acceleratory' substances from the leaves of various plants, especially geraniums, and found that their potency changed sharply for a short period following the Full and New Moon.[76] His research is relevant to the traditional advice that medicinal herbs should be picked at such times.

An important biochemical study was reported in 1989 from the University of Paris. It concerned a lunar pulse in plant DNA.[75] Plant chromosomes, inside the nucleus of every cell, are large, much bigger than in animal cells. Two different types of structure were reported from X-ray studies. One, whose function is more related to storage of carbohydrates, was more developed at New Moon. Another type, more closely related to flowering and growth functions, was more developed at the Full Moon. This DNA response in plants is relevant to the traditional connection of the lunar cycle with fertility and growth.

A plant's metabolism can be assessed by how much oxygen it absorbs from the air. This was investigated in the classic experiments of Professor Frank Brown in which potatoes and carrots were maintained in the dark over quite long periods, with the ambient conditions of temperature, humidity and pressure held constant.[16] Through the years, he patiently charted over a million hours of potato time! From this, it emerged that the potatoes, although sealed from all light, were not at all in the dark about the cycles of the Sun and Moon. The Moon's daily rising and culmination (reaching its highest point in the sky) appeared as the hours of maximum metabolic rate for these root vegetables. In addition, their metabolic rate waxed and waned with the monthly lunar cycle: potato metabolism over the two weeks around the Full Moon was on average fifteen per cent higher than that around the New Moon. For carrots the figure was eleven per cent.

Specific aspects of plant growth may respond to different parts of the phase cycle. An experiment by T.M. Lai, looking at nutrient absorption by corn seedlings according to lunar phase, was reported in the US journal *Biodynamics*.[59] The amounts of potassium and phosphorus, two nutrients vitally important for plant growth, absorbed over a one-week growth period, were measured for six months. The amount of phosphorus which the plants were absorbing peaked at Full Moons and was least during the New Moons. For potassium, this was the other way around. Phosphorus is acidic and root-nourishing, while potassium is required more by flowers and is alkaline (a higher pH), so there is an interesting polarity here.

A growing plant builds up an electrical field around it, in which the electrical potential at its top differs from that at the ground. This was investigated by Harold Burr, a professor at the Yale University School of Medicine. Burr found that measuring such weak electrical fields in humans could lead to better prediction of the time of ovulation in women and an enhanced ability to diagnose the early stage of cancers.[20]

Burr decided to record the electrical potentials of trees by placing electrodes in their trunks.[19] The first thing he discovered was that fluctuations in potential were the same for all trees he investigated over a large area. Surprisingly, these were apparently unrelated to fluctuations in barometric pressure, humidity, or the weather. He then monitored the potential of a single beech tree over a nine-year period, and this clearly showed that the dominant rhythm was tidal, i.e. of 14.7 days, and that it peaked at the Full and New positions. A further analysis of this nine-year experiment was performed by his student Ralph Markson, which showed that the tree's electrical activity was also responding to the level of solar activity (sunspots) but that the lunar cycles were stronger than these solar effects.[20]

Bees are well adapted to the lunar month in their flight activity. Counters were fixed to beehive entrances by M. Oehmke, a biologist at the Goethe University, Frankfurt. Through the course of the year, these showed a huge lunar fluctuation in bee activity.[69] This varied a bit between species, one being at least twice as busy at New Moon as at the Full. Bee activity fertilizes flowers, reminding us of the connection between the synodic cycle and fertility. Surely this matter is just as fascinating as the bee-dance, whereby bees communicate directions for finding flowers to their fellows, even on cloudy days, using the vector of plane-polarized sunlight

At Lyons University, botanist Dr E. Graviou measured the small amount of oxygen which seeds use in respiration when kept in darkness at a constant temperature, when apparently they are quite dormant.[42] With tomato and other seeds she found that maximum oxygen absorption tended to occur bimonthly, at Full and New Moon.

Nowadays, when we speak of a month we forget the lunar origin of this term, and do not consider the life-rhythms in all living things linked to this monthly cycle. No doubt man, in his mechanical environment, responds less to it than do other living things.[30] 'On the days of the Full Moon, something colossal is taking place on Earth,' averred Rudolf Steiner in his 'Agriculture' lectures of 1924, adding the important corollary, 'these forces spring up and shoot into all the growth of plants, but they are unable to do so unless rainy days have gone before.[80] Plants, in spite of man-made changes, still live and grow attuned to this primary cosmic rhythm. The various results reported here show that there operates in plant growth a complex of different rhythms related to the Moon's synodic cycle and that the time of Full Moon is especially important for them. Around this time a plant's metabolic rate and water absorption are at their greatest.

We have seen how laboratory studies indicate that a higher rate and speed of germination is attained if seeds are sown just before or around the Full Moon and, to a lesser degree, if sown over the New Moon; also that seeds and plants absorb water optimally around this part of the lunar month. In countries where drought is endemic this would have some bearing on the success of a crop and may have reinforced the idea that all plants should be sown around Full Moon.

Female Fertility

Many ancient and modern societies believe that women and their biological functions are intimately connected with the cycles of the Moon. The period of human gestation which, from conception to birth averages 266 days, is precisely nine lunar months, reminding us of the mysterious connection which this cycle has with fertility.[25]

The average length of the female menstrual cycle is 29.5 days, i.e. the lunar month, not 28 days as is normally averred. The most common period length is indeed around 27 days but, overall, large-scale surveys have shown the mean to be indistinguishable from the lunar month.[94,97] This is notably so during the peak childbearing years, when the subjects were in their twenties, whereas the mean period length becomes much longer for girls under twenty and is a couple of days shorter for women in their forties.

In general, women with cycle lengths near to the lunar month period of 29.5 days tend to be the most fertile.[26] Also, women tend unconsciously to synchronize their periods when living together.[68] Selecting the sub-group of women with cycles near to the lunar length, between 28–31 days (about one-third of the total), it was apparent that they had a tendency to ovulate at one or other end of the lunar cycle, in other words to have a link either to the Full or New Moons.[25] All these things could imply that the cycle of womankind once had some large degree of synchrony and moved in accordance with the waxing and waning Moon. Then, indeed, the Moon would have been experienced as a fertility goddess. Whether or not this was so, it is a fact that, in ancient societies, agricultural practice did move in tune to the monthly cycle of the Moon[83] and that belief in the power of the Moon to induce fertility and growth was very widespread.

Such findings, and the ancient association of the New Moon with men-struation and the Full Moon with ovulation, led to the expectation that more babies would be born around the Full Moon phase of the cycle, which some modern research has confirmed.[62] After all, ancient traditions linking the Moon with fertility find some support from modern evidence. Such traditions apply equally to the sowing of seed and the fertility of the soil.

Full Moon and Animal Husbandry

> Geld hogs, steers, rams and kids when the Moon is waning.
>
> Pliny, *History of Nature.*

It seems that even nowadays many farmers who have never heard of Pliny's recommendations still follow them regarding castration and other surgery on animals, fearing complications due to excessive bleeding at Full Moon. There is some medical evidence to support this practice. Some years ago a doctor in the United States investigated a group of 1,000 operations which had been performed in his hospital.[4] For all the operations in which complications from bleeding occurred he noted the Moon's phase at the time they had been performed. To his surprise he found that at least four times more occurred at Full Moon than at New Moon. He analysed other groups of operations and obtained the same striking result. From this data it appears that the period around the New Moon is indeed the optimal time for such operations, and that the Full Moon period should definitely be avoided.

Horse breeding

> [Farmers] notice the aspects of the Moon, when at full, in order to direct the copulation of their herds and flocks, and the setting of plants or sowing of seeds: and there is not an individual who considers these general precautions as impossible or unprofitable.
>
> Ptolemy, *Tetrabiblos,* Ch. III

In the Middle Ages, the Arabs were the finest horse breeders in Europe and the Near East. Their subtle understanding of astrology may well have helped them in this breeding process. Then, in the eighteenth-century, Britain out-bred the Arabs, creating the finest racehorses in the world. The UK is presently slowly losing this edge, partly because, with the price of top stallions at several million pounds apiece, they are falling to Japanese and American buyers.

The sex life of racehorses is uniquely documented and published. Nine years of such data were acquired by the author from a thoroughbred studfarm with a throughput of several hundred matings a year. Each mare is covered several times per season until it conceives, though a few per cent remain barren.

Like cows, horses ovulate every three weeks through the breeding season. Veterinary surgeons can tell within 48 hours or so if conception has occurred,

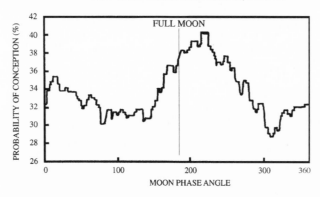

HORSE FERTILITY: FIRST COVERING ONLY
1592 THOROUGHBRED MARES, 1986–94

Figure 7.

therefore the record of mare coverings is a record of their times of ovulation. There is a tendency for horses to become synchronized in their ovulation, hence a studfarm tends to become more busy at three-week intervals. In this horses resemble many creatures in the wild where the females of a species tend to ovulate in synchrony.

Using hormones, vets have unnaturally shifted the season of œstrus (coming on heat) so that it begins in February. Gestation in horses takes eleven months and in the wild they would not foal until May, only dropping their young when the frosts were over. Normally they would be on heat in the summertime.

To analyse this data by Moon phase, only the first covering per mare per season was used, and scored by whether or not conception ocurred. The probability of conception is less than 40 per cent at this first covering. The diagram plots this probability around the lunar cycle (a 'moving average' has been put through the data). It clearly peaks just after the Full Moon.

Thus, three- and four-week rhythms of fertility interact in a horse population, as the mares come on heat in the spring. The former expresses a biochemical cycle within the horses, while the latter responds to the opposition of the two luminaries in the sky. There was also a tendency for horse œstrus to peak somewhere around Full Moon, being then in the region of ten per cent more than at New Moon.

There is a seasonal trend in horse fertility, which makes the Full Moon in June the most fertile time of the year for thoroughbreds. One appreciates that not many readers may have such creatures to breed, but for one's pet gerbil or whatever the same principle should apply.

Harvest Time

Traditions link the time of harvesting crops to the Full or New Moons. One may believe that water and metabolic rhythms connected to this cycle should affect the final condition of a crop. Roman and Greek beliefs on this have already been touched upon. As an instance of modern awareness of lunar rhythms, here is the account of a Sydney-based company on the subject of their tomato harvests (personal communication):

> We are growers of tomatoes, on a relatively large acreage, and found throughout the years that, during the period of the Full Moon, a noticeable change takes place in the maturing and colouring of tomatoes. This quickening maturity, irrespective of temperature, only takes place two or three days before and after the Moon has reached its fullness.
>
> During this period, market places on the east and south coastal states have an influx of coloured fruit where in normal times there is a high percentage of green and semi-coloured fruit. We have tested this out on many occasions and our statistics over many years have shown more fruit passing through our packing house through these periods and that the fruit is much more forward in colour. These conclusions may well echo the experience of many growers.

Such a clearly perceived effect surely reflects the more regular and predictable climate of Australia: one tends not to find so definite a view expressed by British tomato growers.

For crops that are to be dried, where juiciness and high water content is not required, at or just before New Moon seems the appropriate time for harvesting. Thus, the great French herbalist Maurice Messeng always picked his herbs at this time.[67] He dried the herbs before use and believed that their virtue would preserve best if picked then.

Moonstamp for Timber

A related practice which can be traced back to antiquity is that of felling timber at the New Moon. The founder of the US Cycles Foundation in Pittsburgh described how in South America the Moon phase at which timber is felled was stamped on the wood, the idea being that New Moon timber preserves better and cuts more easily than that felled at Full Moon.[28] French law from 1669 until the Revolution specifically required that timber be felled only during a waning Moon, a practice directly echoing the words of the Roman historian, Plutarch:

> The Moon showeth her power most evidently in those bodies which have neither sense nor lively breath; for carpenters reject the timber of trees fallen in the Full Moon as being soft and tender, subject also to the worm and putrefaction, and that quickly by means of excessive moisture.

Accounts of this practice (discussed in Kolisko's *Agriculture of Tomorrow*) give the impression that the effect is more evident in tropical or near-tropical regions. The experience of the Australian Bio-Dynamic farmer, Alex Podolinsky, is relevant:

> There is more water in trees and grass and all plants towards full moon than towards new moon. In the old days good timber cutters chopping down valuable timber would never cut other than towards the new moon. They would not cut towards full moon, the timber was not as good. If we cut hay we also cut as much as possible towards new moon and not towards full moon. We get much better quality hay that way.[73]

On the Trout Farm

It isn't just plants that have their fortnightly rhythms of growth. Trout in an aquarium grow to a rhythm whereby their weight peaks just before the Full and New positions.[37] This was shown using several hundred small trou, and weighing them every four day, as they grew – a commendably simple experiment.

Fish respond biochemically to the lunar cycle. Salmon and some species of trout hatch in fresh water and at a certain stage of their lives transform to become ocean-dwelling salt-water fish. Salmon fisheries need to be able to predict this event, as they have to release hatchery-reared fish into the river shortly before it occurs. The thyroid hormone thyroxine triggers this big moment in the salmon's life and there is a specific New Moon in the spring which precipitates this hormone surge.[41] If the salmon wish to swim down the river without being seen by predators then a New Moon is the optimal time of month for them. This was discovered by zoologists at the University of California who concluded that a lunar calendar was essential for efficient culture of this economically valuable resource.

Back in the 1920s, an American called John Knight developed his theory about when to fish.[58] He posited that fish feed only twice a day when the Moon either culminates (reaches its highest point) or reaches its nadir (lowest point below the horizon). For avid Izaak Waltons, the correct time to indulge their art can be calculated from the calendar below. The time of moonrise each day is given and, very roughly, the zenith and nadir can be found by adding or subtracting six hours from them. Nifty footwork is required to make sure the correct local times are worked out as our calendar is based on GMT.

Knight's theory didn't just apply to fish, he explained. Animals, including humans, would become more active and have more energy at these times than at any other time of day. A recent review of this theory by Michael Theroux concluded that:

As you become familiar with these Solunar periods [Knight's term for daily moonrise and culmination] you will also begin to notice how many other daily events are directed by the moon's influence. Once the connection has been made, there is no turning back.[86]

Power of the Nodes

To remind the reader, the lunar nodes are the two places where the moon crosses the ecliptic each month. We see the ecliptic as a line through the night sky along which the planets move and the Moon's serpent path swings from side to side of this, crossing over it at a node.

Traditionally, the nodes were regarded as powerful energy-points in the Moon's cycle, and large-scale American investigations have confirmed this clearly . At the Washington Weather Bureau, the same team of investigators who discovered the Full Moon peak in rainfall (Chapter 1) also found that the magnitude of the effect varied greatly and depended upon how close the Moon was to a node.[15] The effect was strongest for the Full Moons which happened near to the nodes, and weakest for those farthest away.

A comparable effect on the Earth's magnetic field was found by Bell and Defouw at the Massachusetts Institute of Technology.[9] We all know that the Earth's magnetism points towards the North Pole but, in addition, it fluctuates in magnitude a great deal from day to day; it's a very mutable thing. We have already looked at how it intensified on days after the Full Moon. These

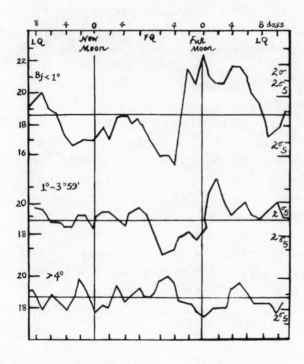

Figure 8. The index of geomagnetic activity according to the lunar phase and the celestial latitude of the Full Moon (after Bell and Defouw, 1966). The three graphs show how far geomagnetic activity peaks at the Full Moon. At zero latitude, the top graph, the variation is greatest. The bottom graph shows the least activity at maximum latitude, i.e. furthest from the nodes.

researchers found that much bigger changes in geomagnetism over the Full Moon occurred when it took place at a node, whereas the effect was hardly present when the Full Moon was furthest from the two nodes. This clearly shows that the nodes affect the power of a Full Moon.

The figure based on their research shows how the GMF (geomagnetic field) peaks at the Full Moon when the latter occurs close to the nodes. There is a disturbance of the Earth's magnetic field of around 30 per cent at this time. This reinforces the idea that the nodes are important power points as well as possibly explaining why the Full Moon is such an energizing time for plants and other organic systems. The effect was much weaker away from the nodes.

There is growing evidence that plants are highly sensitive to changes in the Earth's magnetic field.[31] The biologist Professor Frank Brown found that organisms could detect and respond to small changes in the Earth's magnetic field of a magnitude comparable to those linked to the motions of the Sun and Moon.[18]

Chapter 4

THE MOON AND
CROP YIELD

To speake then of the outward and active knowledges which belong to our English Hous-wife.... Shee shall also know the time of the yeere, moneth and moone, in which all hearbes are to be sowne; and when they are in their best flourishing, that gathering all hearbes in their height of goodnesse, shee may have the prime use of the same.... In February in the new of the Moone shee may sow Spyke, Garlicke, Borage, Buglose, Chervyle, Coriander, Gourds, Cresses, Marjoram, Palma Christi, Flower-gentle, white Poppy, Purslan, Radish, Rocket, Rosemary, Sorrell, Double Marigolds and Time. The moone full shee may sow Anisseedes musked, Violets, Bleets, Skyrrits, White Succory, Fennell, and Parslie. The moone old sow Holy Thystell, Cole Cabadge, white Cole, greene Cole, Cucumbers, Harts Horne, Diers Grayne, Cabadge, Lettice, Mellons, Onions, Parsnips, Larkes Heele, Burnet and Leekes.

Gervase Markham, *The English Hous-wife* (1615)

IN EARLIER CHAPTERS we have looked at many of the influences of the phase of the moon on plants and animal life. Most of the experiments we have reported have related a Full or New Moon to some perceived change in metabolic rate or physical performance. Alternatively, they have investigated the consequences of the relationship of the moon's orbit to that of the Sun, for instance when it crosses the nodes. The moment has come, however, for us to move forwards: to evaluate the importance of the relationship of the moon to the zodiac. This, you will recall, was touched on in our description of the four elements and the sidereal cycle in the first two chapters.

Whereas the phase or synodic cycle is related to the general growth of a plant, it is the sidereal cycle that is mainly linked to the final crop yield. A sidereally-based rhythm applies to one instant in a plant's life, when the seed is sown on moist ground and growth begins. At this critical moment it is the Moon's position against the zodiac which influences the overall development – that is, how the seed's potential will come to fruition.

Systematic investigation of how the time of sowing affects final growth really started with the experiments of Maria Thun in Germany. In 1956, she developed her theory using the procedure of sowing twelve rows of a crop over one sidereal lunar month, usually in May. This method had been followed in investigations within Steiner's Anthroposophical Society since the 1930s, but it was Thun who had the idea of picking out the element-rhythm rather than the separate Moon-zodiac constellations.

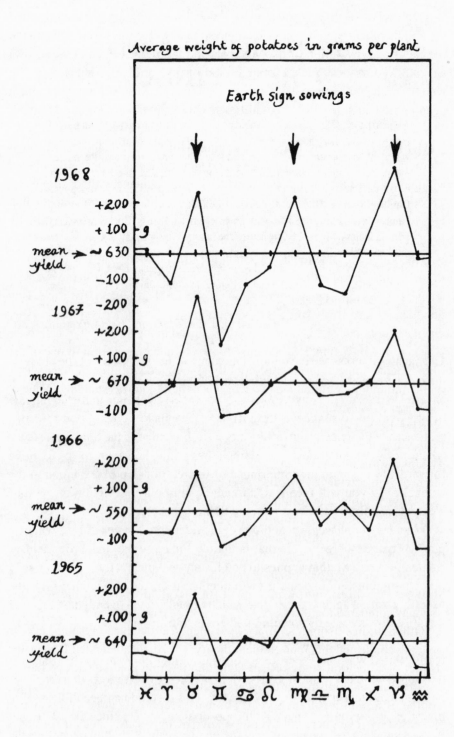

Figure 9. Potato yields according to the experiments of Maria Thun (1979).

One row of seeds was sown every few days, each time the Moon reached the middle of a new zodiac constellation, so that twelve rows were sown in the course of one revolution of the Moon around the zodiac. Each of these rows was allowed to grow for the same period of time and, after harvesting, the weights of the crops from each row were compared. Results for potatoes have been published since 1972 (co-authored with statistician Dr Hans Heinze). Maria Thun has subjected many other crops to the same type of experiment.

Her research garden in a small, tranquil village surrounded by hills near Marberg, Germany, carries on this work. Over the decades she has developed a remarkable insight into the way in which cosmic influences affect crop yield. This may be the only place in the world where systematic research into the link between crop yield and the Moon's position is ongoing. The work was initially funded by a 'research-ring' of German Bio-Dynamic farmers.

The dominant effect emerging from her trials related to a fourfold pattern in the zodiac which allocates each of the twelve constellations to the four elements – Earth (influencing root plants), Water (leaf plants), Air (flowering plants), and Fire (fruit- and seed-bearing plants) – as described in an earlier chapter. For potatoes, maximum yields occurred in the three rows which were sown on root days, that is when the Moon was standing in front of one of the three zodiac constellations traditionally associated with the element Earth, while minimum yields tended to occur when the Moon was standing in one of the Water constellations, in between those of Earth. This pattern indicated the worst as well as the best times of the month for sowing potatoes. There began to appear in the data a basic wave pattern related to the kind of plant sown. The yield increases obtained were in the region of 30 per cent for the three Earth-element sign sowings as distinct from the other nine.

Figure 9 shows the results of the Thun-Heinze potato experiments over 1965–68.[90] Clear maximum yields can be seen over earth-element sign sowings (root days) and minima over water-element sign sowings (leaf days). The results were tested for statistical significance by comparing the mean of the three root-day yields with that of the nine other sowings. Clearly, such a test shows a very high significance level for the yield-excess of the root-day sowings compared to others.

Other studies using a similar experimental procedure as Thun have, in general, confirmed this four-element theory. Ulf Abele at Giessen University, as part of a doctoral study of Bio-Dynamic farming methods, tested barley, oats, carrots and radish over the years 1970–74, sowing twelve rows over the course of a month for each year. His barley and oats gave yields which increased by seven per cent overall when sowings were made on seed days (see Figure 10 overleaf), while his carrots and radish averaged a 21 per cent yield increase on the root-day sowings.[1,2]

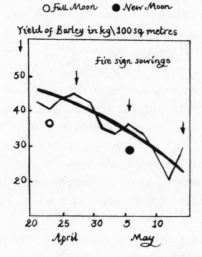

Figure 10. Barley yields according to Abele (1973).

A German study by Ursula Graf investigated the Moon-zodiac rhythm for different soils.[40] Over the three years, 1973–75, potato and radish crops were investigated and yield increases were usually found for root-day sowings as the theory predicted. However, this occurred only in crops grown on organically cultivated soil, to which no chemicals had been applied, and not in crops grown on soil treated with synthetic fertilizer. Graf's conclusion was, 'the soil seems to be a decisive factor in the occurrence of connections between Moon-zodiac constellations and crop yields,' a view which directly echoes Thun's comment in 1964:

> I came to the conclusion that mineralized soils hardly reacted to these cosmic rhythms and their fine influences, whereas a humus-filled soil of whatever soil type was a good mediator for these forces.

In other words, organic gardeners are the only ones who are going to reap important benefits from the calendar and method of working I offer in this book. Soil quality appears very relevant to the way lunar influence will show up and may account for variations in results achieved.

In Britain in 1976, the author and Reg Muntz, a market gardener in Sussex, planted 24 rows of potatoes over two sidereal months.[53] The results showed a mean yield increase of 25 per cent for rows sown on root days as compared to other sowings. Other trials by Muntz involved beans, carrots and lettuce. Maximum yields consistently showed up in the element-trigons predicted by the Thun theory, whereas there was little indication of a lunar phase effect.

Some quite thorough experiments were done in Wales over three years by Colin Bishop, an amateur gardener and astrologer.[12] In 1976, he planted 36 rows of lettuce over three months and achieved the results shown in Figure 11. The average weight of the lettuce tops increased by approximately 50 per cent

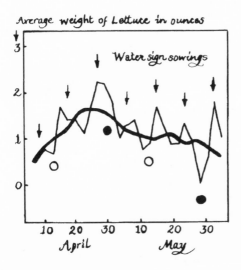

Figure 11. Lettuce yields according to Bishop (1976).

for those rows sown on leaf-days when compared with sowings made on other days. This surprised him. A repeat of the experiment in 1977 produced substantially the same results. In 1978, Bishop experimented with daily sowings of radish and again found that the relevant days, in this case root-days, produced the highest yield by 45 per cent.[55] None of these data-sets showed a Moon-phase effect on crop yields.

There is skill involved in growing rows of vegetables uniformly so that they aren't consumed by birds or slugs and that lettuce form their hearts without bolting. Such uniform conditions of growth are vital for the data to mean anything. Overall, between the years 1975 and 1986, Muntz and Bishop grew some four hundred rows of different vegetables in such trials and, overall, the net yield increase from sowing in the predicted trigons was 22 per cent. The soil used was not especially rich. These British results formed the groundwork for putting forward the calendar you are about to read.

In 1980, J. Lücke sowed four different plots of potatoes, with twelve rows per plot, as part of another doctoral thesis at the University of Giessen, one per Moon-constellation as usual, i.e. 48 rows in all.[63] Overall, his root-day yields were very significantly in excess of the others, just as yields from the leaf-day sowings (opposite to the root-days, as being Water rather than Earth) were the least.

Sometimes a low-amplitude effect is observed, as in the extensive trials designed by Dr Hartmut Spiess.[79] In three years of carrot trials in 1979–81 at Dottenfelder farm near Frankfurt his yields averaged eight percent more on root days, which is not much, but was significant as he undertook many sowings. The plot used was in an industrialized region of Germany where one might expect any sidereal-rhythm effects to become diluted. Some degree of

41

scepticism has developed in Germany over the Thun model, amongst Bio-Dynamic experts, which has focussed on the Spiess results as if they had failed to confirm the sidereal rhythms. I suggest, however, that they are low-amplitude effects rather than null results. Spiess concluded that, 'the magnitude of the yield deviations that were associated with lunar factors was of practical significance.'[78]

For a practical, Australian view of how to use the sidereal rhythms we may quote from the lectures of Alex Podolinsky:

> The market gardeners may have noticed the best beans you have ever picked are on plants that are not huge and have not all that many leaves.... Now if you sow beans under a 'leaf' zodiac sign, then they turn out such huge plants and they have very poor fruit. When you sow under a 'seed' sign, you don't have all that much foliage (the plants don't need it, anyway) but they do have a lot of fruit. For pumpkins, in our experience, sowing under Leo is the most desirable.... We have run such trials and we have had roughly four times as many pumpkins in roughly the same acreage sowing them under 'fruit' rather than under 'leaf'.[73]

A Quality Test

Is the taste of a crop affected by the trigons as well as the yield? Organic growing is about improved quality, after all. Jack Temple, the *Here's Health* organic gardening correspondent, performed such a test in the spring of 1982, using the Thun sowing calendar:

> Every time a leaf-sowing date turned up I sowed a row of lettuce and a row of radishes, and every time a root sowing day featured in her calendar we also sowed both lettuce and radish again. Then, when the directors and students from the Henry Doubleday Research Association dropped in on their yearly visit, we put the trial to the test.

Initially, Jack's visitors were shocked by the outlandish notion so that his reputation with them appeared to be at stake:

> However, all that disappeared as I put my knife through two radishes. One was juicy and the other had the texture of cotton wool. The juicy one had been sown on the correct day, a root-day, and the pithy radish had been sown on a leaf-day. That was not all: the juicy radish was ten weeks old while the pithy one was only eight weeks old. Both radishes were also tasted for quality and flavour.
>
> Subsequently further sowings were tested. Each time we had the same result. Radishes sown on leaf-days were pithy and radishes sown on root-days were firm and fleshy. The lettuce trials did not produce quite such clear evidence, but lettuce sown on leaf days were slower to bolt than those sown on root days.[85]

So, it was shown that the root-day radish had better texture and the leaf-day lettuce were slower to bolt, in front of some fairly critical witnesses.

To date the evidence from such sowing trials demonstrates an effect caused by the primary element-rhythms of the zodiac, but not for specific signs, as if plants, being simpler in their organization than man, respond to this less-differentiated rhythm embodied in the zodiac. The weight of evidence to date indicates that the Thun model is valid and that the final yield of crops, when sown in good, organic soil, is related to the Moon's position according to the sidereal zodiac sign-element at the time of sowing.

Maria Thun has been publishing a calendar to guide organic growers and gardeners for several years. This is translated into several languages, including English. However, it is not able to shake off imitators and plagiarists. In Germany, some half-dozen clones appear in the bookshops each year with a substantially identical calendar and sowing advice to the Thun publication but in glossier covers. 1998 was the first year that one of these imitations appeared, translated into English. These may show that the idea is spreading and help its wider acceptance nonetheless, ethical issues are raised by such copying. I would point out, for the comfort of readers anxious about the abuse of copyright, that the calendar developed for this book is substantially different from Thun's. The reasons for our variations are explained at length below.

There is at present less evidence for the effects of the lunar nodes on plants. According to Thun, the influence of the two nodes is liable to interfere with plant growth and to weaken the viability of seeds from plants sown at these times.[91] The 1977 lettuce experiment by Bishop shows that the three or four rows sown over the Moon nodes failed to germinate. Yields from the leaf-day sowings were on average 54 per cent higher than the others, but the one leaf-day sowing that coincided with a Moon node (14th May) was comparatively inhibited and resulted in a reduced yield.

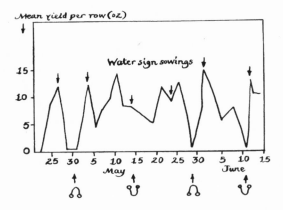

Figure 12. Lettuce yields according to Bishop (1978), with indications of Water (leaf) element days and lunar nodes.

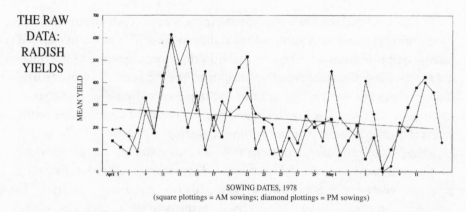

Figure 13. The Bishop radish trial. The root days in this period were April 11–13, April 20–22, April 28 – May 1, and May 9–11.

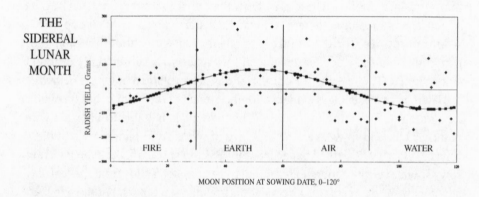

Figure 14. The Bishop radish trial. Here the yield data are plotted against the sidereal lunar longitude (0–120°) at sowing time. The element signs are shown, and a best-fit waveform has been added to make clear the tendency in yields.

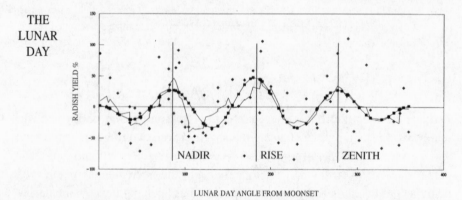

Figure 15. The Bishop radish trial. Here the yields are plotted against the passing of the lunar day. The individual readings have been translated into a waveform and a moving average to better demonstrate the variation in yield according to the time of lunar day of sowing.

At perigee, when the Moon draws nearest to the Earth each month, the tides are pulled higher, some 30 per cent more than at apogee. It has been claimed that perigee is linked with stress.[62] In the 1976 lettuce experiment by Bishop it was found that the highest yield over a three-month period came from a row sown at apogee. Thun has claimed that the apogee position causes sowings to sprout up rather quickly – which may not necessarily be beneficial for fruit formation – whereas the perigee position tends to inhibit growth. Evidence for the supposed adverse effect upon growth of perigee remains scant.

Sowing and Harvesting in the Phase Cycle

Does sowing at some point in the lunar phase cycle (i.e. when the Moon is Full or New, or at a quarter position) produce better crops? Widespread folk traditions have affirmed it, as Moon-gardening almanacs have for centuries recommended diverse Moon-phase rules for the sowing of crops: note, for instance, the suggestions by Gervase Markham quoted at the head of this chapter. Modern experiments have been equivocal, though field experiments by Mather at the John Innes Horticultural Foundation in 1940[64] showed a consistent fifteen per cent yield increase for maize and tomatoes sown in the second lunar quarter, confirming the hypothesis which this gardener had wished to test – that Kolisko had just published in her 1939 *Agriculture of Tomorrow*. Despite this confirmation, the author of the report was quite dismissive of his results, and subsequently a review in *Nature* by Beeson echoed his sceptical tone.[7] Crop-yield sowing trials which Simon Best or myself have seen or been involved in have failed to detect much by way of any Moon-phase effects on yield. A comment by Thun on this issue is of interest, indeed possibly crucial:

> The influence of the Full Moon, throughout all the years of our research, only brought higher yields when these had been forced by mineral fertilizers or unrotted organic manures.

Moonrise

Perhaps the most thorough lunar-gardening experiment ever performed was that by Colin Bishop in 1978, using radish. He sowed two rows in the morning and another two in the afternoon for 38 consecutive days with no gaps. The data is shown broken down by the four elements, the sidereal lunar month, with peaks as predicted on root-days. A waveform has been put through the data to show the star-rhythm. Its amplitude is around 30 percent. Lastly the lunar day angle is shown, centred on moonrise. This graph was possible because Colin Bishop noted the time of each sowing. It shows a large peak over the hour of moonrise. He watered each row before inserting the seed on his way to work each morning and then each afternoon as he returned home. This meant that the seed started growing as soon as it was inserted into the soil. This is important if we are to take seriously the notion that the hour of moonrise showed up as the largest-amplitude effect in this data-set, as here appears.

In the nineteenth century, there was a regular gardening column in *The Astrologer*, a London-based monthly, which always gave the time of moonrise, and recommended it be used for important gardening operations. The calendar we have printed here for you also records the hour of moonrise, even when it is in the middle of the night. My own opinion is that it is a very significant moment in the day when contemplating seed sowing or planting.

Chapter 5

USING THE STAR-ZODIAC

A Doctor too emerged as we proceeded;
No one alive could talk as well as he did
On points of medicine and of surgery,
For, being grounded in astronomy,
He watched his patient's favourable star
And, by his Naturall Magic, knew what are
The lucky hours and planetary degrees
For making charms and magic effigies.

Chaucer, *The Canterbury Tales* (trans. N. Coghill)

LET'S TRY TO TIGHTEN UP the use of the terms 'sign' and 'constellation'. The zodiacal signs are all of 30° length, whereas the constellations associated with them vary greatly, from 46° (Virgo) to a mere 18° or so (little Libra, the Balance, next to Virgo). The calendar here used always employs the equal sign divisions. However, the earlier chapters alluded to the constellations because Bio-Dynamic research always uses them, never an equal zodiac.

In the debates that go on amongst users of Bio-Dynamic calendars, it is generally appreciated that sowing is not advised near the ingress times, so that 'border disputes' over just where a constellation begins and ends are not very important. The irregular constellation divisions used by Bio-Dynamic calendars differ from those here used for one-sixth of the time. That is, some sixty degrees in the circle of the zodiac. This chapter looks at the 'glorious heritage' of the star-zodiac, and argues that the splintered traditions of the twentieth-century calendars can be resolved by an historical view.

The sidereal zodiac, or zodiac of the stars, is composed of twelve equal thirty-degree divisions.[74] It is a kind of 'best-fit' of such a regular structure upon the irregular constellations of the ecliptic. It is called 'sidereal' to differentiate it from the 'tropical' zodiac that astrologers use nowadays. It derives from antiquity, and as such would have been used by the three Magi or 'wise men' of the New Testament: the Magi were astrologer-astronomers of the Near East, chiefly Chaldea, renowned for their star-lore.

In the fifth century BC, the Greek historian Herodotus went to visit the Chaldeans of Mesopotamia. He was mainly impressed by the sheer abundance of their harvests: of grain, figs, olives and vines. Indeed, he was concerned that the account he gave of these things, and of how tall their millet and sesame grew, would strain the credulity of his readers. The Babylonians built an extensive irrigation system using underground piping for their gardens.

Herodotus must have gazed upon the fabled hanging gardens of Babylon, where now is only the dusty desert.

In that period, 25 centuries ago, the Chaldeans began using the zodiac divisions,[98] dividing the sky into twelve equal sectors, to mirror a division of their year into twelve thirty-day months. Did the star-wisdom, for which the Chaldeans became renowned in antiquity, help them in their harvests? Whereas the modern zodiac is anchored to the seasons of the year, with its start at zero degrees of Aries always at the 'Vernal point', for the Chaldeans of old it was fixed by various bright stars.[57]

The Chaldeans were never interested in the Vernal point's position against their zodiac. That was more a Greek notion, and used more for purely astronomical purposes. Rather, the Chaldeans were concerned with what they experienced of the night sky, for example they recorded each time Venus appeared and disappeared from the sky, and perhaps their more experiential attitude could be of value today.

Debates over the star-zodiac's position are over a degree or so.[36] It is important in some contexts but immaterial for a lunar gardening calendar. There were certain stars that fixed the zodiac position, in particular Spica the bright star signifying the sheaf of corn held by the Virgin, around 29° of Virgo. The Chaldean star-zodiac was used by the astrologers of antiquity around the Mediterranean – Greece and Rome, Syria and Egypt – until the fifth century AD. A different tradition then developed in the Muslim Arab world using the tropical zodiac. The two zodiac systems were then only a few degrees apart.

The four elements – Earth, Air, Fire and Water – had been used in Greek medicine and philosophy for seven centuries until, in the second century AD, after Claudius Ptolemy's time, they were absorbed into the fabric of the zodiac. Thenceforth the Lion, the Archer, and the Ram all had one element in common: fire! And, indeed, these three images do seem to have that fiery quality in common. The sky-triangles (trigons) were thus established, linking the four elements. This happened in Syria, where Vettius Valens first recorded it. They entered into the sidereal zodiac and not into the irregularly shaped constellations.

Memory of the sidereal zodiac became lost in Europe but continued in India: the zodiac used there is much the same as that understood by the ancient world. Thus, the primal star-zodiac, from which the modern tropical zodiac evolved, has been in continuous use for over two millennia. It was rediscovered at the end of the nineteenth century, when clay tablets dug up from the banks of the Tigris were deciphered. A sidereal ephemeris was published in 1981 by Neil Michelson of the US Astro-Computing Services. The present calendar uses the same reference as did Michelson, taking the 'Bull's Eye' star Aldebaran as being 15° of Taurus.

In the twentieth century, two incompatible lunar-gardening traditions burgeoned, both ignoring the sidereal zodiac. They offered a choice, of *either* using the tropical zodiac, as used nowadays by astrologers, *or* using twelve unequal constellations, as used in Bio-Dynamic calendars. The former sells about two orders of magnitude more calendars each year (chiefly in the US) than does the latter (chiefly in Europe).

Use of the Tropical Zodiac

The tropical zodiac denotes the Sun's course through the year, that is to say: the Sun will always enter Aries on March 20th or 21st, the Spring Equinox. This zodiac has no connection with the stars! It is related primarily to the seasons. Its only connection to the stars is historical: a long time ago, it was aligned with the constellations. It is the one used in Sun-sign columns in newspapers and by most practising astrologers. It is slowly moving away from the star-zodiac, due to what astronomers call, 'precession'. As I write, it has moved 25 degrees away from the star-zodiac that gave it birth.

In the early 1980s, previous editions of *Planting by the Moon* took a diplomatic view of the way the tropical zodiac might be appropriate for human fate, while emphasizing that evidence pointed to the sidereal as the right one to use for plant growth:

> Incidentally, we are not implying that astrologers should be using the sidereal zodiac for their work. Rather, it seems that different phenomena may be attuned to different systems. The tropical zodiac is a moving zodiac, moving around once every 72 years against the fixed stars, and this evolving system may be valid for man. However, plants are simpler in their organization than man, and have a far longer history, two factors which seem to have inclined their response to the Moon in terms of the more primal and unchanging sidereal zodiac. The position of the Moon in the tropical zodiac requires calculation, whereas its position in the sidereal zodiac can be observed in the sky. Although plants do not respond to the tropical zodiac divisions, it may well be that man's being is more in tune with the special mathematical treatment of time and space on which the tropical system depends..

To put that in simple terms: without an ephemeris (a prepared, printed table giving star times and calculations) could one discern when the Moon was entering into a tropical zodiac sign? Assuredly one could not without a most difficult calculation. If we cannot do it, how could one expect the much simpler plant realm to respond to a tropical ingress? In contrast, growers using the calendar we offer here have the advantage of being able to see in the sky what is happening in the book.

In terms of agriculture, the tropical zodiac reflects the seasons of the year, at least in the northern hemisphere. Thus, the glyph or sign for Aries signifies the young seedling emerging in spring, then the next sign Taurus, the Bull, signifies the vigour of springtime. The Sun's entry into Leo at the height of summer indicates its strength there, followed in September by the Virgin as a Ceres-figure signifying the harvest. After that comes Libra, the Balance, as the harvest is measured out; and then the Scorpion signifies the dying and decomposition of nature.

Interpreting the evidence of field experiments in terms of a zodiac framework depends entirely on the symbolism of the four elements. Thus, experiments show that root crops such as potato or radish grow better when the Moon is in front of one of the three 'Earth' sectors of the sidereal zodiac. In terms of the tropical zodiac, one would have to say that they were growing best when the Moon was in front of one of the three 'Air' signs, because the shift between the two systems is nowadays almost one sign, or 24°-25°. This would not have the same symbolic significance as associating them with the Earth signs. Likewise it makes more sense to associate leaf crops such as lettuce with Water (sidereal) than with Fire (tropical). The four stages of plant growth – root, leaf, flower and fruit/seed – are associated with the four elements, earth, water, air and fire, *only* if a sidereal reference system is used.

Users of this 'zodiac of the seasons', i.e. the tropical, tend to advocate that the three Water signs are fruitful while the three Fire signs are barren, based on straightforward analogy or symbolism. It amounts to viewing only one-quarter of the zodiac as fertile. Sometimes the Earth signs are also admitted to be fertile. Experimental work supporting this view was published by Timmins,[85] which involved sowing only two rows, one supposedly at the right time and the other outside it. This was viewed by Simon Best and this writer as being of doubtful value, on the grounds that one's attitude is too likely to affect the outcome of such a simple and short-term experiment.

Use of the Constellations

Bio-Dynamics developed within the Anthroposophical movement founded by Rudolf Steiner which had drawn up its own twelvefold division of the heavens, loosely based upon the divisions made by the International Astronomical Union in 1928. The astronomers then decided to map out thirteen constellations as lying on the ecliptic (Ophiucus, the Serpent-Bearer, being the thirteenth). The Anthroposophists wanted no truck with this, however, and reconstructed a zodiac of just twelve constellations. Whereas the astronomers saw Libra as being 23° in length along the ecliptic, the Anthroposophists gave it merely 18°, making it even shorter.

The divisions imposed on the heavens by the Anthroposophists had little connection with earlier zodiacs. Whereas both sidereal and tropical zodiacs allocate an equal space to each sign, Steiner and his followers attempted to reflect more closely astronomical reality. The constellations (which is how they divided their calendar) are by their very nature unequal in size.

There was no great harm in any of this, indeed it was quite audacious. The trouble began when Maria Thun stuck the four elements into this irregular setup in the 1950s. Her use of these divisions made for a radical imbalance in the four elements. Root days (Earth) were assigned over 50 per cent more of the month than the flower days (Air). The Air-constellation Libra is very short, while the Earth-constellation Virgo is 46°, two and a half times longer. The system was badly out of kilter, but nobody seemed to mind.

The Sidereal Zodiac

I would ask the reader to put all thoughts of the tropical zodiac, and the variations worked upon it as described in earlier paragraphs, to one side. The present calendar is based upon the sidereal zodiac as being the correct and optimal reference that does really work in an organic gardening setup. Its basis is thus very traditional, tried and tested over millennia. The element-rhythm of the star-zodiac is a simple thing, which is why plants respond to it.

Just as investigation of lunar influence on plants is a recent phenomenon, so also is the rediscovery of the sidereal zodiac in the West. Traditional gardening manuals have used the tropical zodiac without question, largely because it was the only one known to them. With the steady accumulation of evidence supporting the sidereal zodiac framework the practice of lunar planting can now be established on a firm foundation.

Let's check out two sets of evidence for preferring it. First compare the results of the radish experiment by Colin Bishop that was described in the previous chapter, with three graphs to illustrate it. If you recalculate the findings according to the Bio-Dynamic zodiac calendar on the one hand, and the sidereal zodiac on the other, the yields reported by Bishop are as follows (mean weight in grams per radish per row).

	Root days	*Others*
Sidereal:	3.1g (n=18)	2.11±1.5g (n=60)
Bio-Dynamic:	2.8g (n=23)	2.15±1.5g (n=55)

Each of the zodiacs in question is divided into the four elements that we have already discussed, but the unequal division of the Bio-Dynamic tropical zodiac means there are quite a few more sowings on 'root-days' according to their calendar because their three Earth element (Roots) constellations, Bull (Taurus), Virgin (Virgo) and Ram (Aries), are more than 30° in length.

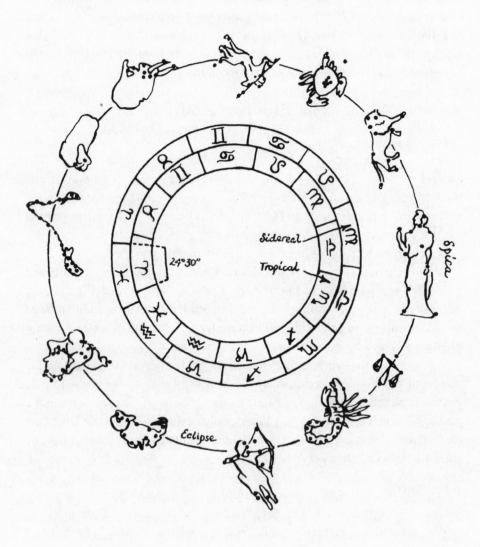

Figure 16. The relationship of the sidereal and tropical zodiacs against the constellations.

Whichever calendar one prefers, the mean yield excess of root day sowings over sowings in other element-signs was over 30 per cent.

A second trial that may be useful for comparing the impact of the two zodiacs concerns goats. One is sometimes asked, did not Maria Thun perform trials herself to check out the validity of the Bio-Dynamic movement's zodiacal divisions? She did perform and write up a fine experiment with goats she milked each morning.[92] For two months, she measured the milk they gave, and then weighed the butter she made from it every afternoon. The goats produced about a quarter of a kilogram of butter each day. A large excess of butter (nearly 20 per cent more) was made on the 'warmth-days', i.e. what the present calendar calls fruit-seed days. This experiment looked at milk quality, not quantity. The total amount of daily milk did not vary greatly, but the amount of butter extractable therefrom varied with the Moon-trigons. Analysing these yields using the sidereal zodiac instead of the constellations (as there are a few days which fall out differently) gave a slightly greater excess of butter yields on the warmth-days than was obtained by the constellations.

If this result turned out to be repeatable then *Planting by the Moon* could start including milking in the calendar recommendations. Readers will appreciate that it would presently be inappropriate to do this – indeed it would be mere intellectual theft (as does happen in certain quarters, but not here).

Seeds of Confusion?

As an example of how the different divisions work, let's consider the figure of Leo the Lion. Tropically, he spans the 30° of 120°–150° (measuring from zero as the start of Aries). Adding on 25° gives sidereal Leo, 145°–175°. Simple, isn't it? For comparison, the *constellation* of Leo is larger, reaching from about 138° to 173°. It can be seen that there is a day when Tropical Leo overlaps the constellation of Leo, bearing in mind that the Moon moves 13° a day.

An American writer and gardening advisor called Llewellyn finds Moon in Leo to be the most barren sign, used only for destroying weeds.' Thun's advice is quite contrary to this. To quote from the US *Kimberton Hills* calendar, Moon in Leo 'enhances the power of regeneration', and is a time for 'sowing crops whose seeds will be saved.' This is the day in each month which one tradition finds to be the most barren and worst for seed quality, while another recommends that, *au contraire*, sowing will produce the most fertile seeds for the future. Days in the calendar with the Leo ingress (boundary) marked in the daytime, for example April 24th 1999, fits the bill. One should cultivate a mood of ironic reflection on such days.

Chapter 6

GARDENING ASPECTS

To the better furthering of the gardener's travails, he ought afore to consider, that the Garden earth be apt and good, wel turned in with dung, at a due time of the year, in the increase of the Moon, she occupying an apt place in the Zodiack, in agreeable aspect of Saturn, & well-placed in the sight of heaven ... for otherwise his care and pains bestowed about the seeds and plants, nothing availeth the Garden.

Thomas Hill, *The Gardener's Labyrinth* (1577)

As viewed from the Earth at Full Moon, the two luminaries, the Sun and the Moon, are said to be in 'opposition,' then two weeks later at New Moon, when they have drawn together in the sky, they form the aspect called 'conjunction'. An aspect is an angle, measured around the ecliptic from the centre of the Earth, expressing some kind of symmetry within the zodiac. Traditionally there were always five of them and, in order of decreasing strength, these are:

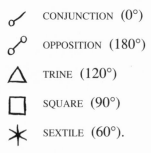

CONJUNCTION (0°)

OPPOSITION (180°)

TRINE (120°)

SQUARE (90°)

SEXTILE (60°).

The conjunction, square and opposition are usually considered inhibiting and stressful, whereas the sextile and, in particular, the trine are thought to be beneficial and harmonious.

Each month, the Moon forms similar angles or aspects with Saturn and with the other planets. The relationship thus expressed with Saturn seems to have particular importance to agriculture and the life of plants. The present calendar indicates most of the Moon/Saturn aspects as they occur, a certain number of Moon/Sun aspects where they are relevant and all the aspects between the Moon and Venus when they fall on Flower days. The Venus aspects are here being recommended for working with flowers – sowing, planting-out and grafting.

Aspects to Saturn

The planet Saturn was traditionally viewed as important for farmers. The Roman god Saturn presided over agriculture (his name is thought to derive from the Latin *sator,* sower) and the Saturnalia, held just before the winter solstice, was a week-long agricultural festival of merry-making, in memory of the Golden Age. Indeed, classical writers have mentioned no other planet in this regard. In his agricultural poem *Georgics*, Virgil advised, 'Watch the transit of the cold star Saturn.' Saturn's sickle had a more rustic meaning before it came to denote the limitations of time.

As an example of this traditional view, the sixteenth-century work on gardening lore, *The Gardener's Labyrinth*, explained about sextile aspects between Saturn and the Moon: 'it is then commended to labour the earth, sow, and plant,' whereas, during the square aspect between these two, it was 'denied utterly to deal in such matters'. The trine was also approved, but the opposition was not.[44]

Much the same advice featured in seventeenth-century British works, for example *The Whole Art of Husbandry*,[65] while *Dariotus Redivivus* advised that farmers:

> ought to have a special respect to the state and condition of Saturn, that he be not ... afflicted, because he hath chief dominion over husbandry and the commodities of the Earth; let him therefore (if you can so fit it) be in good aspect ... to the Moon.[27]

For planting crops, the general advice was, 'Plant what you intend, the Moon being either in conjunction, sextile or trine of Saturn.'

In modern times, Bio-Dynamic farmers have considered the lunar opposition to Saturn to be important, so that it was for long the only celestial aspect to feature in their calendar.[11] It is here interesting to note that the Foundation for the Study of Cycles, based in Pittsburgh, has found a 29.8 year cycle in famines,[28] a periodicity which corresponds almost exactly with the average time it takes Saturn to make one complete revolution through the zodiac. (Incidentally, there are no other planetary revolutionary periods near this time-period; the two closest to Saturn, Jupiter and Uranus, having periods of 11 years and 84 years respectively.)

In astrological terms, Saturn represents life's challenging, defining and shaping principle. It can be depicted as *Chronos*, 'Old Father Time'. The present calendar gives the lunar aspects of conjunction, opposition, trine and sextile to Saturn. For those who wish to test these aspects, the traditional advice would be that the harmonious times are suitable for the sowing of perennials and trees, through Saturn's association with long-term cycles, and for increasing the hardiness of plants. Stressful times (conjunction, opposition and square) should be avoided but readers may wish to test the particular belief of Bio-Dynamic farmers that the opposition is the best Saturn aspect to use. All aspects are given to the nearest ten minutes GMT.

One should sow or plant between one hour before and half an hour after the aspect occurs. That was what *Planting by the Moon* has earlier advised. If that seems unduly strenuous, one could quote Adele Barger's view, in *Gardening Success with Lunar Aspects*, 'sow within the six hours prior to exactitude, taking care to sow before and not after the event.'[6] The present calendar gives Saturn aspects for leaf, flower and fruit/seed days, but not for root days, as there would be little point in sowing trees and perennial crops on root days.

In his ever-popular herbal, Culpeper gave some advice about when to pick herbs in terms of finding the right celestial aspects, adding:

> Let them be full ripe when they are gathered, and forget not the celestial harmony before mentioned; for I have found from experience that their virtues are twice as great at such times as others.[22]

Vines and the Sun

Readers with a warm and sunny spot in the garden may wish to try growing vines; with all this global warming, why not? For the ancients and for traditional astrological-rustic books the vine had a *solar* rulership. The US biologist-astrologer Lee Lehman compared rulerships of all sorts of herbs and trees from a variety of traditional sources and she found a nucleus for which all of her sources agreed. The vine was one of these. Most of these don't concern us as planetary events are not given in the calendar which follows in this book (it would be too complicated). However, the main Sun-Moon aspects are given and these are the important options for choosing when to establish a vine, particularly cutting the scion in the autumn and then grafting it in the spring. Such times should also be a fruit-day. Such days occur on 18 December and 25 April.

The ancients also related wine quality to the movement of Jupiter around the zodiac. As it orbits once in twelve years, it will enter a new zodiac sign each year. Various astrologers that I consulted expressed surprise about the solar rulership of the vine. They never guessed it, expecting it to be ruled by Jupiter. The words jolly, jovial, joy and so forth derive mysteriously from that sphere in the sky: Jove. This is something to mull over. One might also seek for solar aspects to Jupiter or Venus (not given in this calendar) for the important and career-determining event of setting up a vineyard. As not many readers are likely to be doing this it is a somewhat theoretical issue.

To help understand this idea, let's quote from a recent book on plant rulerships by Jean Elliott[33] which brought Culpeper's *Herbal* up to date. She gave the grapevine as solar in its rulership and summarized solar qualities as follows:

> The Sun: Core essence, integrated conscious self, playful self, vitality. Play, children; palaces and mansions; day; gold. The Sun rules Leo. Colour: yellow, orange, gold

> Grapevine: (*Vitis Vinifera*). Lilly, Culpeper [referring here to the two seventeenth-century astrologers who gave rulerships]. Either grows as a long-lived climber or in bush form for wine. Green/white flowers from early to midsummer. Grapes in Autumn. Under 'Vine' in *Herbal*. Brought to Britain by the Romans.

Fifteen years ago, one of the most respected French wine estates, Clos de la Coulée de Serrant in Savennières, owned by Nicholas Joly, went Bio-Dynamic.[45] Under azure skies in the Loire valley, there are two wines now produced using a lunar calendar: Joly's and Noel Pinguit's Le Haut Lieu. This last has won every award going (described as 'a stunningly intense, joyful wine' – solar qualities, perhaps?). One per cent of French wine is presently produced according to a Bio-Dynamic regime.

Joly expresses his views in rather solar terms:

> When we look at a flower or fruit, it becomes perfectly clear that they owe their beauty, their colour, their fragrance, their variety of shapes and flavours to the sun. And it is precisely this power of expression, which manifests itself in constantly new variations that must again be allowed to flourish in wine – and in every foodstuff.

Readers tired of Euro-plonk will surely appreciate this comment:

> Our apparently progressive agriculture has largely destroyed the soil as a living entity. As a result, the soil is now hardly capable of sustaining growth. It has consequently become dependent on chemical fertilizers, which are inevitably absorbed into the vine itself… In the past, wine growers enriched the soil whereas nowadays, they feed the vines directly. This amply explains the ever-increasing uniformity of wines available from the retailer.[30]

As the grapes ripen a critical situation develops in the last few weeks, crucial for final quality. The grapes have to be collected at their optimal stage of ripeness. As acidity gradually decreases the sugar content rises. After harvesting they are crushed and the mix poured into barrels. That moment needs careful choosing, being the 'birth-moment' of what will mature into wine, so make sure it's a fruit-day.

Maria Thun is collaborating with a wine-grower in the south of France. When I went to visit, her research plot of vines was being treated with various sprays of different copper concentrations. Copper sulphate is regularly sprayed as an insecticide, but she was using higher dilutions of copper, in other words much weaker concentrations along the lines of homeopathic medicines, to investigate their efficacy in the battle against infestation.

In 1988, the Domaine de la Romanée-Conti, producing the most famous red Burgundy of all, announced its decision to go organic, which caused a sensation. In 1995 they formed an association for compost production in an endeavour to revitalize the soil.

1990, the last sunspot maximum, is regarded as a classic wine-year. We will shortly reach a new sunspot maximum. As the Sun expands, with solar flares extending further out from its surface and aurorae maximizing at Earth's poles, are the best wines then formed? To quote from Gauquelin's classic, *The Cosmic Clocks*:

> According to the French Astronomical Bulletin, years in which the number of sun-spots is highest are great vintage years for Burgundy wines; in years with few sun-spots poor vintages are produced. The Swiss statistician A. Rima found similar results when he analysed the production of Rhine wines for the past two hundred years .

Karen's Pear Tree

The great astronomer Johannes Kepler composed calendars that prognosticated for the year ahead and in one of them (1602) he explained how it all worked.[39] He described an early version of the 'Gaia' theory, whereby 'the earth has a vegetable-animal force, having some sense of geometry.' This sense of geometry, he explained, enabled it to respond to the celestial aspects, in terms of climate, harvests, good wine years and political stability. Kepler gave an analogy to explain how this worked: just as a peasant could take delight in the piping of a flute, without knowing anything about the theory of musical harmony, so likewise did Earth respond in an unconscious manner to the changing geometry of the heavens. Earth more or less shuddered during an eclipse, he wrote:

> eclipses ... are so important as omens because the sudden animal faculty of the Earth is violently disturbed by the sudden intermission of light, experiencing something like emotion and persisting in it for some time.

Early tablets from ancient Babylon testified to the belief in the infertility of the land around the time of an eclipse. As a belief, it has endured longer than most. The early Bio-Dynamic sowing-calendars by Franz Rulni advocated not sowing anything important for several days after an eclipse, while its sucessor, the modern Thun calendar, gives just the day of an eclipse as no-planting.

In Holland, there is a garden with a few ragged pear trees which only started to bear small, bitter fruit nine years after they were planted. They were planted under a solar eclipse by Karen Hamaker-Zontag, the eminent Dutch astrologer. As a test, she planted them at this inauspicious moment. One would like to see an agricultural college sowing some fruit trees over a solar eclipse, with others growing on adjacent ground for comparison's sake that were planted at some more favourable time.

That eclipses do in fact diminish seed quality was shown a few decades ago in a series of seed-germination experiments by Theodor Schwenck summarized in his book, *Sensitive Chaos*. Readers unfamiliar with this work have a treat in store.

Chapter 7

THE RHYTHM OF THE SUN

THE SUN IS DUE to reach its next peak of sunspot activity in March of the year 2000. This is expected to damage or knock out all sorts of satellite communication equipment and to overload power grids, causing several billion dollars worth of damage. Experts are predicting that it will be one of the worst (or best, depending on your viewpoint) ever. It will cause Earth's upper atmosphere to expand as it is heated up, affecting low-orbiting satellites…but, our concern is with a very different field, namely its effect upon living things.

If you look at rings in an old tree trunk sawn across, you will notice that some are wider than others, a measure of increased growth during certain years. Usually, it can be seen that these widest bands happen every eleven years or so. The beat to which they and a host of other life forms keep time is that of the changing level of solar activity, as indicated by the number of sunspots visible on the surface of the Sun.[68] The sunspot cycle peaks on the average every eleven years, though it can vary. The solar magnetic field, north-south of the ecliptic, reverses every twenty-two years. This longer period comprises the complete solar cycle.

The cause of these thicker rings is something many millions of miles away: a heartbeat inside the Sun itself. The origin of this pulse remains a mystery, but its cycles are carefully followed by counting the spots and flares observed on the Sun's surface. Sunspots are a barometer of solar activity. Figure 17 shows recent cycles with 1959 and 1980 the highest on record.

While lunar rhythms define optimal sowing days within one season, this grand pulse of the Sun determines the years of peak production and also lean years, linked with times of famine. This expansion and contraction within the Sun affects rhythms of total crop production and much else besides. Experts

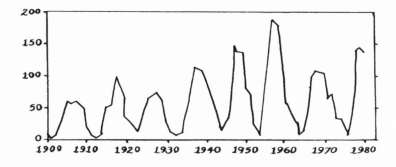

Figure 17. The solar cycle, sunspot activity 1900–1980.

generally assume the influence is indirect via the Sun's effect on climate: electrical and magnetic changes in the upper atmosphere are caused by solar radiation, these affect the climate, which in turn affects crop yield. The subject has implications for economic forecasting and may eventually come to be used for this.[47]

Ever since the astronomer William Herschel stated, two centuries ago, that the price of wheat varied with the sunspot cycle, scientists have been arguing whether the effect is really present. Meteorologists at the Appleton Laboratories at Slough are one group to have researched the subject, and their conclusions were quite positive. Led by Dr J.W. King, they found that, in Britain, yields of potato, turnip and swede tended to peak at years of sunspot maxima and also that rainfall tended to increase during these years.[48]

The scientists further found that the number of days per growing season (defined, somewhat arbitrarily, as days whose mean temperature was above 6°C) increased markedly during years of peak activity.[49] This confirms the observations of an English farmer, Mr Farrar, reported in *Farmers Weekly* in 1975, that the length of his cows' annual grazing season varied with the sunspot cycle. From his family records, he found that over the decades his cows stayed out to graze longest in years of peak sunspot activity, presumably when grass was blessed with an extended period of growth.[38]

The effect of the sunspot cycle on temperature was also found for the US states Maryland, Delaware and Virginia during the years 1900–60. Mean variations of two to three degrees centigrade linked with the solar rhythm – although this correlated primarily with the complete 22-year cycle rather than that of eleven years. This has obvious relevance, Dr King argued, for energy budgeting.

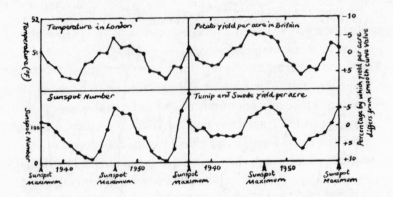

Figure 18. Variations in temperature, sunspot activity, and yields of potatoes, turnips and swedes through two complete sunspot cycles. (After King et al., 1974.)

Rainfall is also linked to the sunspot cycle. Dr R.G. Vines in Australia found that years of drought in certain countries are linked to troughs in the sunspot cycle, and large forest and prairie fires occur more often in these years.[96] He counted bad fire years as those in which losses overall due to fires were of one million acres or more. It is perhaps not surprising that fires on Earth should be linked to rhythms in the fiery energy of the Sun. Major US droughts seem to remain in step with the 22-year rather than the 11-year cycle.

Can farmers expect bumper harvests in years of sunspot maxima and more meagre yields in years when the Sun is quiet? Quite a lot more research needs to be done on Sun-Earth links before such recommendations are likely to be made by agricultural scientists, but it may not be long before farmers take account of this solar pulse when planning ahead.

The effect is geographically dependent, with wheat prices shown to correlate strongly with this cycle in some parts of the world, whereas in others such a correlation is lacking. In countries in the southern hemisphere the cycle is clearly reversed, with least growth in years of sunspot maxima. In general, Dr King and his colleagues found wheat yields in the northern hemisphere increased in years of peak sunspot activity, causing global wheat prices to be lower then because most wheat is grown in this region. Their research indicated that: 'Modulations of 10% to 50% of the wheat production in China, the United States and the Soviet Union seem to be correlate with the solar cycle.' Dr King suggested, as others have done before him, that this could be used as a basis for global economic planning.

Other phenomena have been shown to vary with the Sun's cycle, for example, years of peak activity seem to produce good wines. This appears both for French Burgundy and for German Rhine wines. The Russian expert, Professor Alexsander Chizhevsky, studied this cycle in human history, claiming that more political upheavals, unrest and warfare took place in years of peak activity. Russians regard him as the founder of Heliobiology.

Nowadays, the people having a practical interest in the cycles of the Sun are radio and electrical communication companies. This is because they get more disturbance and interruption during times of solar storms. RCA employs experts to monitor the Sun's activity. Farmers too, let us hope, will find it to their advantage to take account of this mighty pulse at our system's centre.

As long ago as 1937, anthroposophist J.W. Stein postulated 'the solar and planetary influences on weather and climate as the foundation of harvest and prices'.[52] He discussed such phenomena as temperature and rainfall linked to this cycle, emphasizing how much the effects were geographically differentiated. Further studies have confirmed what Gauquelin wrote in 1964, that, 'the relation between the sun and the atmosphere is as complex as that between the two main characters of a psychological novel'.

When the Moon blots out the Sun during a total eclipse, and the sky grows dark, then the red rim of the solar chromosphere appears around the edge. This chromosphere, in years of sunspot maxima, will glow all around the Moon, during a total eclipse, whereas in quiet years of sunspot minima it is seen to glow only at low solar latitudes, each side of the Moon's black rim. This means that the Sun's chromosphere expands and contracts over the 11-year cycle, though normally it is invisible, and only seen during total eclipses. Over the August solar eclipse of 1999, near to the sunspot maximum, astronomers will be keen to check out by what degree the deep-red solar chromosphere has expanded.

The Nutation Cycle and Long-Term Planning

Long-term rhythms and recurrent patterns are not confined to the Sun. Every planet will have some kind of cyclical relationship with the Earth. In the 1980s, reports started appearing of the 18.6-year lunar-node cycle being identifiable from climate and agriculture records. It is now viewed as being at least as influential as the solar pulse. The word 'nutation' means a wobble, as this cycle causes Earth's axis to move. The axis of the earth takes many thousands of years to move round against the stars, and added onto this is this relatively small gyrating movement every 18.6 years, which astronomers call 'nutation'. This may help us understand the huge effects which this cycle exerts upon Earth's biosphere, at least as strong as the solar cycle: it moves the axis of the Earth. The solar cycle may be more evident in northerly countries, where a greater flux of energized solar particles, as shown for example in the aurora borealis, can funnel down from the Van Allen belts into the atmosphere. Rainfall or drought are linked with this node or 'nutation cycle' in several parts of the world. The monsoons of India, tidal waves – aqueous or atmospheric – and the nineteen year cycle of flooding of the River Nile are instances that may be cited.

The US cycles expert, Dr R. Currie, has found that droughts in midwestern states seem to follow the 18.6-year node cycle.[23] It affects atmospheric tides which in turn influence the flow of rain-bearing air. This region, where much of the world's grain is grown, is known to suffer severe droughts approximately every 20 years. High-yield periods in the US, nearly free of drought, tend to occur near minimum declination. The 'El Nino' weather pattern, a global reverberation affecting atmospheric perturbation, droughts and many other climatic factors, appears strongly linked to this same nodal cycle.[45] Currie has found both lunar and solar cycles, that is to say of 18.6 and 11 years, present in the atmosphere, the lunar signal being stronger than the solar.[24] For example, he has traced the 18.6-year lunar node cycle through floods and droughts in China for the past five centuries and these measurements and his conclusions have serious implications for food production worldwide.

In times to come, these two long-term cycles will come to be used in economic forecasting: the nutation cycle of 18.6 years and the 22-year solar cycle. In both cases, one-half of the cycle can often appear as the effective length. For comparison, the cycle of the lunar month causes a fortnightly peak in the tides. Astronomically, the lunar 'declination', which relates to how high the Moon rises in the sky, varies with the 18.6-year nutation cycle, while half of this cycle is 9.3 years, in which eclipses revolve around the seasons of the year, as there is no difference between the north and south nodes in this regard. A 9.3 year cycle in US grain production and prices was discussed by Thompson, with high yields occurring in years of minimum declination.[87] In the US, lowest agricultural prices tended to occur every 18.6 years.[88] Currie has also argued that a crop production cycle of 18.6 years exists. This confirms the conclusions of Dewey and his Cycles Foundation who identified cycles in wheat prices that ran for either nine years or 18–19 years.[28] US pig, chicken and egg production also varies with the node-cycle: 100,000,000 more US chickens are produced at the peak than at the trough[24] – the largest lunar influence yet identified! The study was extended over the half century 1910–60. [87] Herschel's original comment on corn prices and the rhythm of the Sun, therefore, may today be adjusted to match a lunar, not solar rhythm.

Chapter 8

THE ORGANIC WAY

Clear the sheds of dung, but not at new moon or half moon.

Cato, *On Farming*

THIS CHAPTER IS LESS an explanation of the beauties of lunar gardening, more by way of a call to all readers to embrace plant and food production along organic lines. I may be preaching to the long-since converted who may wish to skip to the next chapter. But many pay lip-service while dipping the knee to another master. These may care to listen again to a rehearsal of the arguments.

Organic farming took off during the 1980s, during which period the number of UK organic farms increased sevenfold. There are presently in excess of 700 farms certified organic and rather less than ten per cent of these are Bio-Dynamic. The movement has appeared as a largely northern and middle-European phenomenon. Nearly ten per cent of Austria's cultivated acreage is organic; Denmark and Sweden are not far behind. In Germany, over two per cent of farmland is designated organic and France comes a close second with just under two per cent. By contrast, the UK has only one-third of one per cent of its cultivated area classified as organic! However, if measured by the number of farms or the total acreage, the UK is fifth in the European league table.

At last, official support is being voiced for the organic movement. In May 1988, the Minister of Agriculture admitted in a parliamentary statement that,

> I am keen to encourage organic farming as a sustainable farming system that can contribute to environmental objectives and can, in particular, deliver real benefits to bio-diversity, while producing a product that the consumer wants and is prepared to pay a premium for.

It is an indication of the swing in public opinion that the Ministry of Agriculture, Food and Fisheries (MAFF) now makes available grants to assist farmers during the difficult two- or three-year conversion process, before an official seal of approval (usually from the Soil Association) enables crops to be sold as 'organic'. That said, the grant is little more than token. MAFF also funds research into organic systems at Elm Farm, Berkshire. Every week now *Farmers Weekly* has an organic grower's column, and that is quite a change.

In 1993, an EU regulation established a legally-binding definition of organic food. Let's hope this will suffice to block dire new US legislation of 1998, permitting such things as genetically-modified, additive-treated and irradiated materials which would negate the meaning of the word organic. 1998 was also the first year in which food generally available in supermarkets contained genetically-modified foodstuffs *without* consumers being informed. Sixty per cent of processed food contains soya products, two percent of which comprises the new US genetically-modified soya.

Genetically-modified tomatoes last longer on the shelf, and no doubt genetically-modified vegetables will be more resistant to the poisons which farmers spray so liberally upon the land. However, it is far from evident that such developments will have *any* benefit to the consumer. For US agribusiness to railroad the use of genetically-modified soya without even having to label the package is a frightening indication of the shape of things to come. Readers may wish to ask the manager of their local supermarket whether they stock organics, how much of their food has been irradiated, and what position they have on genetically-modified products? The answers will doubtless be unsatisfactory.

In case any reader is confused, irradiated food does not mean it is radio-active but merely that it is dead. Wheat will normally germinate, but that which has been irradiated will not. Nothing will happen if it is moistened. So the arrival of these new technologies poses quite urgently the question whether any kind of life-energy exists in food, and how far the organic farming movement should be committed to such a belief? In using a lunar-gardening calendar, you are surely expressing an affirmative reply to this rather central issue.

In the past, organic farming has sometimes been defined ,rather negatively, as being free from the herbicides, pesticides and fungicides of the chemical industry and innocent of inorganic fertilizers (NPK). Organic growing appeared as mere romantic reaction by ageing hippies who were striving to recapture a lost rural idyll. Reality was that chemicals were needed to feed the world. All that has now changed, with huge food surpluses from over-production. Farmers are paid to set aside productive land. It is a positive advantage that the organic way involves a slower rate of growth and a lower final crop yield.

The bible of organic growers has been Nicolas Lampkin's *Organic Farming.*[60] The Soil Association's journal is called *The Living Earth*, which is for consumers, whereas growers might read *New Farmer and Grower*, Britain's journal for organic food production. There is also a wonderful new Euro-book, *Organic & Wholefoods, Naturally Delicious Cuisine* (expensive), which does have some quite positive comments upon Bio-Dynamics.[30]

Research in animal husbandry has made it plain that animals fed on organic diets are more fertile. One survey found that all fertility parameters for rabbits, such as litter size, were enhanced by an organic diet. Also, rabbits fed on chemically-produced foodstuffs were found to be more prone to disease. With human male fertility apparently continuing a long-established tendency to plummet this should be a matter of rather central importance.

Let's say it loud and clear: organic farms don't have BSE (Bovine Spongi-form Encephalitis). To be more specific, cows born and bred on organic farms do not have BSE. Indeed, Bio-Dynamic farmers received quite a fillip when a a statement made in 1923 by Rudolf Steiner was unearthed: if cows were fed on meat produce, they would go mad.[81] And so they did.

A five-year study published by the US Department of Agriculture found that organic farms had yields roughly equal to, and costs considerably lower than, conventional farms.[95] The organic farms were found to use more labour per unit of produce but to consume less energy. With increasing shortages of energy the importance of this hardly needs stressing.

Panels of tasters tend to prefer organic food. Also, organics have longer shelf-life. The concept of quality is being refined by these and other investigations and should be of great relevance for future studies of lunar influence. We are moving towards a positive definition of what 'organic' means in terms of taste and other characteristics, not just the absence of chemical products.

There may be progress but still hedgerow removal continues; still only two per cent of the population works on the land; still the large-scale concepts of agribusiness and its awfully bogus concept of efficiency tend to prevail; and yet farmers continue to have the highest suicide rate of any profession, a full double the national average, due partly to social and work-induced isolation, partly to loneliness, partly to immense financial pressures and never helped by a lack of esteem amongst the predominantly town-dwelling public. But an organic farm may knit the community together, particularly when it endorses the concept of Community-Supported Agriculture. Young people hanging around the streets could be tossing bales of straw, collecting eggs from the chickens and making hedgerows.

Organic farming puts more people on the land, is more labour-intensive, *but* it gets more produce from the land per acre. Shops selling organic produce presently import 70 per cent of their vegetables from Europe, chiefly Holland. There, public subsidy contributes more to the equation than it does in Britain. Surveys show that over 50 per cent of the British public want more support for organic farming. Indeed, demand for organic food is increasing at over 20 per cent a year. With less than one per cent of UK farmers being organic there is a long way to go. The new official UK Register of Organic Farms keeps the facts and figures and will give helpful advice. For a farmer deciding to make the big transition, there is nothing more reassuring than having an expert turn up from Elm Farm.

Readers may well be interested in investing with a bank such as Triodos which supports organic agriculture and local community projects in return for a marginally lower interest rate. Originally this was a Dutch bank but is now based in Bristol. A next step for town-dwellers is to subscribe to a box-scheme, whereby organic vegetables are available or delivered to their door weekly. If one subscribes near the beginning of the year, the overall cost works out as little more than ordinary shop produce. Such a scheme gives one an experience of participating in the cycle of the year. Seriously, would you trust a tomato in January? A box scheme gives one vegetables as they come off the farm and you too may experience the country-person's 'hunger gap' when the fields are producing nothing more than a few roots before the flush of spring crops is ready.

A few stalwart readers will wish to spend a week or so on a Bio-Dynamic or organic farm – a chance to become totally exhausted, gaze at lovely countryside, converse with like-minded people, tune into Nature's rhythms, sleep like a log, work with appropriate-scale technology, taste more delicious food than one can remember, and ruminate on lunar cycles. There are about fifty Bio-Dynamic farms in Britain now.

As well as waterproof boots from Army Surplus, one should take a star map for the month, as this could be the only opportunity of the year to view the Milky Way, due to the creeping scourge of light pollution. Fewer and fewer townspeople ever get to gaze upon the glittering majesty of that starry wheel. Lie down on the grass at midnight GMT in the summertime and just gaze. Somewhere up there lies the Galactic Centre, with the Scorpion and the Archer on either side ...

One may notice two respects in which Bio-Dynamic farms differ from other organic farms.[11] Firstly, the cows have their horns on, reminding one of the line in Virgil's rustic poem:

Glittering Taurus opens the year with his golden horns.

The horns express the dignity of the cow, as being that part of it which faces upwards. The highest concentration of gold in the cow is in the horns. In the human body, by comparison, the highest concentration of gold is around the heart. The cows have to be given enough space, so they are safe with their horns. There is something wonderfully mild about a cow, as if it had no idea of the harm which it could inflict with its horns. A farmer who leaves the horns on the cows is worthy of respect in the community.

The other difference lies in the use of a lunar calendar. 'We can't sow now, as the Moon isn't right,' I was first told in 1970 (at Tablehurst Farm in Forest Row near Ashdown Forest) and the question haunted me thereafter. Franz Rulni produced his first Bio-Dynamic calendar in 1948, followed later by the Thun calendars from 1963 which continued the difficult task of linking the cycles of Earth and Sky.

Nowadays, not only are cows fed with steroids, milked by machine and deprived of horns, but they don't even get sex. Semen, after being cryo-genically frozen in liquid nitrogen, is just injected. Farmers select the genes of the bull of their choice. What kind of view of Creation is this, to assume the dumb creatures can be so treated without repercussions on us?

The sidereal rhythms that I describe in this commentary and the calendar which follows are likely to work best for the gardener using organic methods. Research indicates that good organic soil produces crops healthy enough to respond well to these cycles, whereas that to which fertilizers are added may not, or at least not to the same extent. Such organic soil, ideally, is built up over the years with compost and is humus-rich, with well-rotted manure – its organic matter digested into a dark friable humus. If, on the other hand, inorganic fertilizers are relied upon, these will force the growth of plants, initially increasing quantity but not quality, and decreasing storage life, disease resistance and, eventually, soil quality.

Using the rhythms of Mother Earth is one aspect (but nonetheless a vital one) of organic gardening. In contrast to the high cost of agro-chemicals and their long-term effects on soil productivity, organic methods offer both a safer and more cost-effective alternative.

I take courage from a better gardener than myself, Jack Temple, who writes the organic gardening section for the magazine *Here's Health*. His columns were collected into a book, *Gardening without Chemicals*.[84] He would now and then assure readers that sowing by the correct Moon-element made a big difference, even, say, for cress grown indoors: it was worth waiting a few days until the leaf-days came round, he reckoned, even if it meant storing the cress in the fridge for a while.

Jack was keen on putting calcified seaweed into his compost preparations and also rock phosphate from Chile. This latter is an 'inorganic' chemical but one on the Soil Association's approved list because it is slow-release. Indeed, some gardeners don't like using it on the grounds that it is too insoluble.

After harvesting a vegetable plot Jack wouldn't dig. Organic kitchen waste was spread across, so were any vegetables the local shops were throwing out, then cut grass and nettles were added, with a dusting of calcified seaweed, and it was all covered with cardboard, empty cartons, and finally black plastic sheeting so that no weeds could grow. Worms and insects munched their way through beneath this until, in the spring, the soil was friable and ready for the next crop. The taste of his vegetables was an experience.

Once, a row of his beans was infested by blackfly. 'Needs some more compost,' Jack remarked. He was proud of his worm compost. What connec-tion compost application was supposed to have with blackfly infestation was far from clear to me but it was applied and the next week, lo! the blackfly were gone. There was an irrigation stream around his plot which provided enough frogs to control the slugs.

He seemed to have the right attitudes towards harnessing the forces of nature to the ends of man: ingenious, yet with proper respect.

Chapter 9

REMINDERS FOR THE VEGETABLE GARDEN

I: A Repertory of Plant Types

IT IS USEFUL TO HAVE a list to hand of which sort of plant belongs to which element or sign. The calendar itself is not filled with detailed instructions about which plants to tend at any particular time, but merely which *type* of plant. Every gardener will have their favourites and an infinity of space could be occupied with redundant suggestions.

 WATER
LEAF PLANTS

Alexanders
Angelica
Asparagus
Basil
Bay
Brussels sprout
Cabbage
Cardoon
Celery
Chervil
Chicory
Chinese cabbage
Chive
Claytonia
Coriander
Cress, American
Dandelion
Dill
Endive

Fennel
Florence fennel
Good King Henry
Grass
Hyssop
Kale
Lamb's leaves
Lavender
Leaf beet
Lemon balm
Lettuce
Lovage
Marjoram
Mint
Mizuna
Mustard and cress
Orach
Oregano
Pak choi

Parsley
Pennyroyal
Purslain
Rhubarb
Rocket
Rosemary
Sage
Salad burnet
Saladings
Seakale
Sorrel
Spinach
Summer savory
Tansy
Tarragon
Thyme
Winter savory
Wormwood

EARTH
ROOT PLANTS

Asparagus
Beetroot
Carrot
Celeriac
Chinese artichoke
Garlic
Hamburg parsley
Horseradish

Jerusalem artichoke
Kohl rabi
Leek
Liquorice
Mushroom
Onion
Parsnip

Potato
Radish
Salsify
Scorzonera
Shallot
Spring onion
Swede
Turnip

AIR
FLOWERING PLANTS

Artichoke
Bergamot
Borage
Broccoli
Broom

Calabrese
Cauliflower
Chrysanthemum
Cowslip

Elderflower
Marigold
Nasturtium
The flower garden
Violet

FIRE
FRUIT & SEED PLANTS

Apple
Apricot
Asparagus pea
Aubergine
Blackberry
Blackcurrant
Broad bean
Cherry
Chilli pepper
Courgette
Cucumber
Damson
Fig
French bean

Gooseberry
Gourd
Grains
Greengage
Loganberry
Mange-tout pea
Marrow
Medlar
Mulberry
Nectarine
Pea
Peach
Pear
Plum

Pumpkin
Quince
Redcurrant
Runner bean
Squash
Strawberry
Sugar snap pea
Sweet corn
Sweet pepper
Tayberry
Tomato
Vine
White currant
Worcester berry

II: A Plan of Work

Ken Whyatt, who has spent many years using organic methods, has kindly provided this excellent and practical seasonal guide to organic vegetable gardening throughout the year. I hope it will prove useful to the reader, even though climates may not be quite the same as for Ken (51°N, south-west England).

January

Burn woody rubbish in a slow smother fire. The resultant ash, when sieved and mixed with leaf-mould in equal parts, will make a wonderful base for sowing seeds later on. Keep the ash in a dry place. If clods of earth are stacked round the bonfire, these will crumble and make a useful ingredient in a potting mixture for tomatoes later in the spring.

Spread compost on vacant land, to remain until the soil is suitable for making seed beds. Inspect all vegetables in store and safeguard against hard frosts by covering with straw, matting or other light, dry material.

Make a cropping plan for your plot, making sure that cabbages (and members of the cabbage family) and potatoes are rotated – planted in an area not occupied by these crops for at least two years previously.

Order seeds in good time. Early seed potatoes should be chitted – placed in trays in a light, frost-free place so that they may develop short green shoots – thus gaining several weeks' growth at planting time. If your soil is a sticky clay, do not walk on the garden unnecessarily unless it is frozen. Keep a supply of old planks to put down to walk on to pick sprouts and other winter crops in wet weather. This will ensure that your soil will be easier to dig in the spring.

If you have a sheltered area facing south and the soil is well-drained and crumbly, sowings may be made of early peas and broad beans (long-pod varieties). Cloches will give added protection. Shallots may also be planted, provided the soil is not sticky.

February

Lightly fork over the area intended for sowings of early carrots, lettuce, cabbage, beet and parsnips. Incorporate well-rotted compost or leaf-mould and sieved bonfire ash in the top two inches. If the soil is too sticky to rake to a fine tilth, keep it covered with cloches for a week or so. Small sowings may be made of early peas, short-horn carrots, lettuce, summer cabbage and Brussels sprouts.

Delay sowings of parsnips and beet (Boltardy is recommended) until late in the month. Even then, beet will require the protection of cloches. These seeds are large and can be spaced about two inches apart. A small sowing should provide salad beet in June if the spot chosen is a sheltered one.

Parsnips should be sown at intervals of about nine inches in rows eighteen inches apart. Seed must be fresh and it is advisable to sow in groups of three or four seeds to ensure even germination, the weaker plants being thinned out in April. To ensure the rows are well marked (parsnips are slow starters) sow radish about one inch apart in the same rows. These will be ready for pulling long before the parsnips have grown large.

Jerusalem artichokes may be planted about 12 inches apart. Remember they can attain a height of six feet so they can be used as a wind break, shade for late sowings of lettuce and as an excellent vegetable in their own right, provided they are properly prepared and cooked.

The main sowings of broad beans may be made now. It is worth planning to succeed broad beans by a crop that requires plenty of nitrogen such as cauliflower, autumn cabbage or broccoli. The beans' roots increase the soil's nitrogen content. When the crop has been picked, cut the haulm to ground level and leave the roots where they were.

March

A busy month if the weather is kind. It is better to wait until the end of the month before sowing than to sow on pasty soil. Broad beans are a worthwhile crop, but must be given plenty of room to develop. Pinch off the top six inches when they are in flower – the shoots make a delicious salad or cooked vegetable and the plants are less liable to attack from blackfly.

Sow main-crop Brussels sprouts, cabbages and short-horn carrots for summer use; celery or celeriac and leeks in seed boxes in garden frames or greenhouses. Plant out lettuces from February sowings, ensuring they have plenty of compost in drills directly under their roots. Further sowings of lettuce should be made from now throughout the spring and summer. A pinch of seed will sow a short row of about four feet and this will suffice if sowings are made fortnightly. The same rule applies to radish, which are large seeds and can be dropped in a drill singly about an inch apart.

Onions can be purchased as sets – normal onions whose growth has been arrested in the autumn. These are planted in fine soil manured for a previous crop. Just push them in the soil without bruising them and cover their necks. As they start to root they may push themselves out of the soil. Replant them with the tip of a trowel.

Parsnips may still be sown, but should be in by the end of the month if they are to attain maximum growth.

Peas may be sown in continuation. The taller kinds will need the support of twigs or netting and the rows should be far enough apart for ease in picking. Rows of lettuce or radish can be sown as catch crops between the peas at the same time, as these will mature before the peas are ready and will benefit from some shade.

Fine soil with plenty of compost is needed for a good yield of early potatoes. If these have two or three green shoots already formed (see January) they can be planted towards the end of March. Spinach, spinach-beet and Swiss chard can now be sown, the last being the most useful, its thick, fleshy midribs making a separate dish from the large spinach-like leaves.

Annual weeds, and even perennial ones, will wilt in the sun if the surface is hoed slightly. They may look unsightly for a while, but worms will assist in clearing them, and the dying material will act as mulch.

Continue to plant out Brussels sprouts, cabbages, savoys and broccoli. There is still time to plant marrows and cucumbers outdoors if plenty of humus is available to give them a good start.

Leeks may now be planted from seed beds. Trim about an inch off the leaf-tips and trim back straggly roots. They are then dropped in holes made by a dibber about eight inches apart and watered in without pressing back the soil.

Runner beans and tomatoes will require strong stakes, which are easier to push in if the ground is first soaked. Plant after the stakes are in position.

April

Tomatoes can be sown in late March, but plenty of light and an average temperature of 60°-65°F is necessary for a good start, so early April is soon enough. Minimum requirements are a warm window-sill not subject to draughts, a good seed compost in boxes of two-inch depth, and thin sowing. When the seedlings are about two inches high they should be planted in separate three-and-a-half-inch pots and grown until early May in a warm, light place before moving to a cold greenhouse. Do not plant outdoors until late May or early June.

A useful plant is land or American cress, similar in appearance, taste and food value to watercress. Sow in a damp spot such as the north side of a low wall, or close to a concrete path, where it is easy to keep them watered.

The main sowings of dwarf beans, beet, broccoli, spinach, autumn and winter cabbages, carrots and herbs of various kinds may be made this month (bearing in mind that dwarf beans are frost-tender, so these could be delayed to late April or even May). January King cabbage and the varieties of purple and white broccoli are useful winter vegetables which will withstand hard frosts when greens are so expensive to buy. Incidentally, broccoli and Brussels sprouts need an open situation and at least two feet between plants, with a good firm soil. Wind tends to rock them, so draw up some surrounding soil from time to time to hold their stems firm.

Early and maincrop potatoes should be planted before the end of the month, giving the maincrops a minimum gap of two feet in the rows and two feet six inches between the rows. If the early potatoes have come through the soil, earth them up slightly and cover with soil if frost threatens. Periodically, they should be earthed up leaving a curved rather than a sharp ridge.

May

Take the opportunity during dull, showery weather to plant out seedling cabbages, cauliflowers and Brussels sprouts. Plant to the base of the lowest leaf-stalks and make the soil really firm. Thinnings of lettuces may be planted out, but ensure the roots are not damaged. They must be thoroughly watered, unless the weather is showery, and prefer a spot with some daytime shade.

Runner beans, courgettes, marrows and ridge cucumber are all sown this month, but must have some protection from late frosts. Cloches are ideal for this and home-made polythene frames or tunnels ensure a good start. Close up the ends with a sheet of glass, as wind-tunnels are not appreciated by any plant.

Early May is the best time for sowing maincrop beetroot, the thinnings of earlier sowings being useful raw in salads. Pick them when they are the size of a golf ball.

Late broccoli, savoys and winter cabbage such as the excellent January King are sown this month. Swedes and turnips are useful as a winter crop and should be thinned to eight inches apart when one inch high.

Capiscums sown in the middle of May, given sufficient warmth, will provide green pods in the autumn. It is not too late to sow carrots; in fact, the later sowings are less prone to attack from carrot fly. Incidentally, when thinning carrots for salads, remove the tops to the compost heap and tread back the soil loosened in the rows. The fly is attracted by the smell of carrots and likes to lay its eggs in loose soil.

Keep cauliflowers well watered with diluted liquid manure. They are the hungriest and thirstiest of plants, although celery must run them very close. This vegetable is naturally a ditch plant and does well in a trench with soil banked on either side. These ridges are useful for catch crops of lettuce or radish; when they have been gathered, the soil is used for successive earthing up of the celery for obtaining well blanched stems.

Sweetcorn needs a sheltered, moist spot. Sow the seed to fill a square rather than in rows. This assists pollination.

Peas can still be sown, but it's a good plan to leave the finished seedbed, after raking it over, at least two inches below the surrounding soil. Water can then be given in plenty.

In the third week, tomato plants for outdoors should be hardened off. An improvised polythene-covered frame will suffice until the plants are put in their final quarters early in June.

June

Dwarf and runner beans may be sown for a continuation of supply or if previous sowings have failed.

Lettuces will bolt if planted out in sunny positions. It is far better to sow thinly, using any thinnings for salads. Afternoon shade provided by taller plants will lengthen the growing season.

Water will be required by most vegetables if rainfall is light: if it has been standing in tanks, so much the better. Always give a thorough watering; the effect of dribbles is to bring roots to the surface, only to be left high and dry. An all-night drenching from a sprinkler hose will do wonders to beans, lettuce, beet, celery and cauliflowers during a dry spell – if the state of the nation's water supply or the depth of your pocket, if on a water meter, permit. In fact, plants benefit from evening soakings far more than any in the morning; the morning is a good time to add a mulch of lawn mowings before the sun can bake the surface of the soil. Mowings will gradually disappear as earth worms take them down, thus helping to aerate the soil and increase its fertility.

July

Complete planting of cabbages, savoys, Brussels sprouts, broccoli and leeks. Swedes and hardy turnips can still be sown in the south of England. Spinach beet and Swiss chard can be sown for next spring cropping. Repeatedly pinch out side shoots from tomatoes, except bush varieties. Harvest shallots and onions as they ripen and keep runner and dwarf beans picked as soon as they are large enough. Beans must never be allowed to grow coarse or they'll become unproductive.

Sow winter radish and thin to six inches apart. A sowing of parsley in a sheltered spot should withstand the winter. Dig early potatoes if ready. Keep the soil moist, remembering that showery weather is usually a good time to give a crop a soaking.

As plots become vacant, for example after onions have been harvested, it is a good plan to dig the soil, incorporating leafy vegetable rubbish and compost in shallow trenches as the digging proceeds across the plot. Woody waste such as cabbage stems are best disposed of on a bonfire, the plant ash being collected and kept in a dry place.

A sowing of a suitable variety of spring cabbage may be made in northern districts during the last week of July. In the south, this is best deferred until the first week in August. Care in selection of a variety suitable to the district is advisable, this being one of the most valuable crops to be grown.

Cucumbers, marrows and beans will benefit from good soakings of rain-water warmed by the sun. An excellent liquid manure can be made by chopping nettles or comfrey into rain-storage tanks, allowing them to soak for a few days. Tomatoes, in particular, benefit from this liquid, supplemented by a dressing of wood ash round the roots and followed by a mulch of lawn mowings. The plants will make rapid growth and set their trusses of fruit early.

August

A problem with sowing seed at this time of year is the likelihood of the soil being too dry; it is not advisable to water seeds *after* they are sown. This may be overcome by drawing a drill rather deeper than normal, soaking this and sowing on top, finally covering the seeds with fine sifted soil mixed with leaf-mould or peat. The dry layer above the seeds will prevent rapid evaporation, keeping the seeds moist enough for quick germination. This method works well with seeds sown in August, such as onions, lettuce, winter radish and spring cabbage. If, however, drought conditions prevail, a soaking from a fine sprinkler or a can with a fine rose can be followed with a light covering of hedge trimmings. These will soon wilt, but will prevent caking of the surface, Alternatively, cloches may be used after the watering, the cloches being lightly covered with hay or prunings for a day.

From spring until autumn grass mowings not required for mulching should be rotted down on a compost heap. Layers of grass, not more than two or three inches thick, should be interspersed with garden and kitchen waste. Rotting will be faster if smaller quantities of animal manure are spread between layers and a dusting of lime is added from time to time. Good composting is an art in itself and there are many publications which deal fully with this subject. Suffice to say here that there is no finer material for plant feeding than a well-rotted compost. Spread as a mulch between crops or on vacant plots as a weed smother. Worms will be active in the autumn incorporating this material into the surface far more effectively than the gardener can ever do by digging it in.

Pick cobs of sweet corn while still green. Harvest onions as soon as the tops have died down. Continue to pick tomatoes as soon as ready. Surplus beans freeze well.

September

Sow varieties of lettuce that have been specially developed for over-wintering under cloches.

Continue to lift potatoes and maincrop carrots. Store sound roots for future use. Do not leave these vegetables in the ground when they have reached their maximum growth for slugs and other pests can do much damage.

September can be the worst month for weeds, many of which are hurrying to ripen their seeds for the autumn winds to scatter. Remove them to the compost heap where the warmth generated by lawn mowings should destroy them. Vacant plots can be utilized by filling (but not overcrowding) with cabbage, winter lettuce and spinach plants.

In dry spells, celery can be earthed up a few inches at a time. The stems will then be blanched. Plant out winter lettuce in land manured for a previous crop. On heavy soil it is advisable to plant on top of a slight ridge to avoid damping off. A further sowing of a winter-hardy variety may be made.

Use parsley as required from the seedling rows, leaving strong plants standing about six inches apart. Cover them with cloches if the plot is exposed to cold winds in the winter.

If your garden is exposed, or in a frost pocket, it is as well to prepare for a slight frost towards the end of the month. The risk is greatest during clear anti-cyclonic weather and the morning sun does the damage. Have polythene sheets or even newspaper handy to drape over tomatoes and peppers. They can be removed after an hour or so. Another way is to spray the plants with cold water. Gather ripened marrows for storage in a dry place.

Sow lamb's lettuce or corn salad. This is an invaluable salad which can be used during the early spring when lettuces are scarce and expensive. Cut like spinach.

October

Continue to pick tomatoes as they ripen and, if frosts are imminent, remove whole trusses of fruit to ripen in trays lined with newspaper. They will ripen in the dark providing they have warmth. The whole plants can be lifted, complete with roots, and hung in a cool greenhouse for the remaining fruits to ripen or they can be used green for chutney. With some care, it is possible to have ripened tomatoes until Christmas.

Dig the remainder of maincrop potatoes; they are liable to slug infestation if left in the soil. Ensure that the minute, undeveloped potatoes are removed, otherwise these can grow next year, possibly spreading disease to both tomatoes and potatoes. Parsnips may be dug as required but will improve if frosted and may remain in the soil until wanted. Beetroot and carrots will not withstand hard frosts and are better stored in dry sand or peat in a cool place.

Put annual weeds on the compost heap. Put tree leaves in a separate heap as they take much longer to rot. Keep the garden tidy, removing yellowing leaves of the cabbage family and other decaying matter which only harbours slugs and other pests in the garden and is far better on the compost heap. Heavy land should be rough dug during the autumn and given a good dressing of compost. Light soil is best composted in the spring.

Spring cabbages are planted this month. If two varieties have been sown, so much the better. They should be firmly planted, closer than other cabbages, say twelve inches apart in rows two feet apart. In spring, alternate cabbages may be cut, leaving the others to grow larger.

A final sowing of winter-hardy lettuce can be made early in the month, covering with cloches. Celery should be earthed up during dry spells and celeriac lifted as required, the remaining roots being covered with dry soil to protect from hard frosts.

November

Clear up fallen leaves and put in a heap. Chicken netting will prevent them blowing about and the resulting leaf-mould can be used at the bottom of next year's potato drills.

It is a good plan to turn semi-rotten compost, placing the outside to the middle and the middle to the outside of the new heap. When completed, give a sloping finish, dust with garden lime and cover with old matting to keep off excessive rain.

Woody waste, potato and tomato haulms and diseased plants should be burnt in a slow smother fire, if possible covered with clods. The ash and burnt soil can be sieved when cool, kept dry and used in sowing composts next spring.

Continue forking over vacant land and burning perennial weed roots. Leave the surface rough, or cover heavy land with rotted compost. A light forking is all that will then be necessary in the spring to prepare the soil for planting and sowing.

Jerusalem artichokes can be used as wanted and some stored in sand for use during hard frosts. Clear out all roots as they are dug. Even small pieces will grow next year and can become invasive. If horseradish is grown the same advice applies.

On dry soils, a sowing of broad beans will repay the effort by producing a finer crop than those sown in the spring. If land is in danger of becoming too wet the roots will rot. Cloches help prevent this.

Corn salad or lamb's lettuce thrives in a dry, sheltered spot and is most useful in early spring salads. Sown early this month under cloches it should provide plenty of tender green stuff in April.

December

It is better to dispose of soft vegetable waste in winter by digging it into trenches during the rough digging of vacant plots than to put it on the compost heap where vermin may be a problem.

Plan ahead for the coming year, making a list of crops which bear well on your soil and ensuring that they will be planted in proper rotation. Leaf vegetables do well on soil previously used for bean crops because of the latter's nitrogenous deposits created by bacteria from nitrogen in the air. Potatoes, if well manured, provide a well-dug soil suitable for beans and peas the following year. Roots can follow members of the cabbage family – give a scattering of lime prior to sowing; but keep lime away from land required for potatoes, otherwise scabby skins will result.

In a four-year crop rotation of this sort, lettuce, tomatoes, celery, leeks and onions can be fitted in where they are likely to do best; but it is advisable to move onions and leeks around from year to year.

III: THE EIGHTEENTH-CENTURY GARDENING YEAR

This is an edited extract from a grand cookery and household manual written by Mrs Martha Bradley and published in 1756 called *The British Housewife: or, the Cook, Housekeeper's, and Gardiner's Companion*. Martha Bradley arranged her work in twelve monthly instalments and at the end of each part she included a couple of chapters on the vegetable garden, flower garden and orchard. She was perhaps a more expert cook than gardener and most of her material seems to have been drawn directly from one of the most influential eighteenth-century manuals: Philip Miller's *Gardeners Kalendar*, first printed in 1731.

The reasons for printing this version here range from its intrinsic interest, to the fact that old gardening practices are often of current relevance, especially to people who are trying to give up sprays, chemicals and other toxins. Martha Bradley's ideas make a nice counterpoint to the more up-to-date suggestions of Ken Whyatt, above.

Martha Bradley did not include much about fruit bushes (gooseberries and currants) or soft fruit, nor did her idea of orchards extend far beyond beautifully espaliered stone fruits like peach and apricot.

Central to the internal economy of the Georgian vegetable garden was the dung-powered hot-bed. It fulfilled much the same role as the modern green-house for forcing early crops. I have omitted some of her instructions where they revolved around technicalities of dung selection and supply. For rather similar reasons, I have left out the paragraphs about raising melons and cucumbers. They were preoccupied mainly with hot-bed management: useful for maybe two or three people today.

In the instructions which follow, where she does refer to hot-beds, the modern gardener may think in terms of plastic or glass cloches or frames. Where there is doubt about a plant variety or name I have included a note in square brackets. Not everything she says or does will find favour today. She plants potatoes in February and harvests them in November; she sows crops very early. Some of her apparent anticipation of the spring and summer derives from the use of hot-beds, some from having well-protected walled gardens that had warmer or colder borders in them depending on orientation. These borders were played upon by the skilled gardener with an almost musical virtuosity.

These much-edited extracts do not include the recommendations about the flower garden made by Martha Bradley. The difficulties of relating old varieties and nomenclature to modern usage would make reproduction so burdened with notes and qualifications that it would constitute almost another book in itself.

January

This is a season at which very little is produced in the garden or orchard, and very little is done in them. What can be done this month will in a great measure depend upon the weather. If very hard frosts continue the ground will not bear working and all that can be done is to get things in readiness against its will. If it be a little milder, the beds are to be dug up for spring crops and you may sow radishes, carrots, lettuces, spinach and young salading, as well as Windsor beans.

Celery should be blanched, and the mushroom beds well covered to preserve them from the severity of the weather. Endive [*where she refers to endive she means the curly endive or chicory, not the Witloof chicory as is grown in Belgium*] may be transplanted and new asparagus beds earthed up if there be shoots. Cauliflower plants are also to be carefully watched [*against frost*].

A gentle hot-bed may also be made for raising mint, as also carrots and some other roots, to be transplanted out when the weather permits for early service. Some peas may also be sown in warm and sheltered places.

Where there are espaliers, this is the time to mend and repair them with new poles and good fastenings wherever they are loose. The earth is to be dug about old fruit trees and it will be very proper to dig in some old and perfectly rotted dung about them. At the same time, dig and prepare the borders for young fruit trees. Grafts for early fruits are to be cut at this time and laid in the earth in a warm, dry place.

If the weather prove moist, this is a good time for cleaning the old trees of moss and cutting off the dead branches, making the stumps smooth and even. Hardy fruit trees may also be pruned at this season. The roots of new planted trees are to be defended from the cold by mulch and the fig trees should be covered with a reed fence or with mats.

February

Most of the summer crops are to be sown this month, therefore let there be great care taken not to lose the opportunity. The mildest weather is best and is always to be seized upon. Sow leeks and onions, carrots and parsnips, cabbage lettuces and spinach. Begin now, and sow a small parcel again before the end of the month. Young salading is sown now in warm borders. Sow at the latter end of this month scorzonera, salsify, and skirrets [Sium sisarum, *a species of water parsnip, grown for its root, once widely eaten in England*]. Cauliflowers to be sown on moderate hot-beds; plant in open ground shallots, rocambole [*Spanish garlic or sand leek, used for flavouring dishes*], chives and garlic. Plant out some cabbage plants, particularly the sugar-loaf kind. Sow peas and beans twice this month so that the crops may follow [*to get succession*]. New beds should be made for asparagus. French beans should be sown at the end of the month on a moderate hot-bed. At the end of the month plant out cos lettuce where they are to stand; some cabbages and savoys are sown now for winter use. Celery should be sown now in a warm rich border; potatoes and Jerusalem artichokes should be planted. Finally, let the garden be well looked over for snails and other vermin and all killed that are to be found.

The hardier kind of fruit trees are now to be pruned and towards the end of the month some of the more tender kinds. All kinds of fruit trees are to be transplanted into the places where they are wanted; if the weather be favourable towards the end of the month, pears, plums and cherries may be grafted. Kernels of stone fruit may be sown, and in moist weather the moss should be pulled off from fruit trees and the greatest care is to be used to keeping off mischievous birds. Among these the principle and worst of all is the bullfinch. One week in the latter end of February, when the weather is mild and favourable, is often of more consequence than three at any other season.

March

It is a season in which much is to be done and he who would acquit himself to his own credit and his master's satisfaction must every day be busy. If there be any planting unfinished, it must be immediately undertaken; if apricot, peach and nectarine trees are left unpruned, let it be done without more loss of time. There will be some early blossoms in this month and the curious may shelter them to preserve them from the perpendicular fall of dews. By this means blossoms that would otherwise have been destroyed by these dews and frosts will set. Yew, holly, box, and the like may now be removed to where the gardener pleases, observing to open a hole large enough for them and to throw in well broken earth, and to see it well settled about their roots.

This is a very good season for grafting and inoculating. Towards the end of this month the fig trees are to be examined and all the old wood that can be spared is to be cut away as close to the stalk as possible for this does not bear. The bearing wood on the fig tree is principally the last year's shoot, these are therefore to be preserved. The beginning of the month is the best time for pruning cherry, plum and peach trees of one year's growth.

About the middle of this month look to your strawberry beds. Dress up the beds with a little fine manure, water them thoroughly. Clip away all the runners till they blossom. Plant out cauliflowers in a good warm bed. Uncover the asparagus, spread some loose mould about them and a little fresh manure. Plant out asparagus roots into new beds. Keep up a succession of salad plants by sowing fresh parcels once a week on warm borders. Sow cabbages and savoys for a winter crop, and celery for early blanching. Sow cardoons [*first cousin to globe artichokes, grown for their fleshy stalks or midribs, the plant is blanched before harvesting – see instructions below*] which are then transplanted towards the end of April. Globe artichokes must now be dressed so that you have three or four suckers on every strong root. The others should be slipped off carefully for transplanting. Sow lettuces, beets, fennel, chervil, spinach, dill, burnet and sorrel. Sow endive thinly. Divide tarragon roots and plant eight inches apart. Divide and plant out chives. Sow purslane and nasturtium on hot-beds. Continue sowing radishes, cabbage lettuces for soups and cos lettuce for salads. Continue sowing peas and beans for succession. Set out hardy sweet herbs such as mint, balm, penny-royal, savory, thyme, sage, and tansy. Parsnips and carrots should be sown, and onions, borage, bugloss. Sow Hamburg parsley in drills a foot apart in rich deep earth. When they are ready to be thinned leave them eight inches apart. Thin the early spinach beds: plants about four inches apart. Sow French beans in light and fine soil.

April

Put your last hand to the fruit trees to prepare them for the summer's service. The pruning and nailing, if any part be defective, must be supplied and finished with a very tender hand, for it is too far advanced for such operations. Look carefully for the last time and see if any dead wood escaped your eye. Cut it out with a sharp knife and a steady hand. Water those trees that have been planted this spring or autumn if the season be dry. Lay a heap of stones around the bottom of every new-planted tree. This answers two purposes: keeping the earth moist about the roots, and keeping the tree steady. Some content themselves with laying weeds or straw about the roots, but this answers only half the purpose. Watch the shoots of new-planted trees, rub off such as grow ill. Cherry trees that are in danger of being hidebound are now to be eased by slitting down the bark in such places with a knife. It is remarkable that the grain of cherry bark runs circularly, so that this method is sure to relieve them.[*This practice can be likened to that of whipping walnut tree trunks to release the tight grip of slow-growing bark and allow them to put on a spurt of growth.*] Let the vines be watched this month and all useless shoots removed; and the suckers be taken from the roots of fig trees.

Let the gardener now clean his alleys and lay all in order in his kitchen garden. Sow beets, sorrel, parsley, onions, and chibols [*spring onions*]. This is a very good time to sow French beans. Choose a dry soil and warm border and sow them in shallow trenches two feet apart, the seeds at four inch intervals. Rouncival peas [*a particularly large variety*] are to be sown as well as other peas and beans for late crops. Lettuce should be sown to succeed former crops. Purslane and nasturtium should be sown to take their chance in the naked ground. Water the strawberries every three days if the weather is dry: the fruit will come in such abundance as very well to repay the trouble. Cardoons to be sown directly where they are to grow: place four seeds in a hole made with a stick, make these holes at five feet distance. When the young plants come up keep the strongest and pull up the rest from each hole. Hoe the carrots and parsnips to destroy weeds and thin the plants. They should now be left about eight inches apart. Do the same to onions, leave four inches apart. Transplant young celery plants into beds of deep rich earth. Place about six inches apart. Water lightly until they take root. Hoe between the rows of beans and peas. Draw up the earth round the stems of cabbage and cauliflower plants.

This is the best season for propagating rosemary and lavender and the like by cuttings. Observe that cuttings of rosemary succeed in this way just as well as slips and do not hurt the mother plant in taking them off, whereas the slips tear and make wounds that do not easily heal. Many a fine shrub has died from this the next winter when the cause was forgot and the damage laid only to frosts.

There is no season at which the garden is so overrun with vermin.

May

This is a month when the sun has a great deal of power, and if there happen some rain, as there generally does, especially towards the beginning of it, a great deal of care must be taken in every quarter to keep down weeds. The useful crops will be at this time growing stoutly: but if they be not cleaned from weeds their progress will be checked and they will be backward and poor. Continue sowing all kinds of young saladings: they should be sown once a week or oftener, for they grow quickly too large for use. As to their situation, that should be now just the contrary to what it was to be early in the spring. Then they required a warm south aspect, now they should be set in a northern border, for the season favours them so much.

This is a very good season for endive: let it be sown for blanching. First it is to be thinned, for it will rise too thick; afterwards it must be kept very free from weeds. Purslane may now be sown upon a good warm south border in a sheltered place. This herb is too much neglected; it is wholesome as well as agreeable to the palate. If you intend to have late crops of beans, sow some in the third week in May upon the coldest and dampest border of the garden. Peas may be sown for the same purpose in the same manner. Choose a good, rich, moderately warm border for a second sowing of kidney beans. The cabbage and celery sown in April will now be of a height to plant out. Water them for the first three or four days. Prepare a bed for winter cauliflowers. Sow the seed carefully and defend it from birds. Lettuce of several kinds will now demand nice care in their management. Remember that, besides the present crop, there must be a succession. While continually drawing some for use, sow and transplant others. Where early cauliflowers begin to show the first signs of a head, break down two or three of the innermost leaves to cover the flower. This will preserve it white and make it grow thick and hard. Look over the early cabbages. They will begin to round. To assist this, tie the top leaves together with string. It makes for a better head which will be whiter and harder. Remove artichoke suckers. Sow turnips and broccoli. When turnips come up, thin them to stand a foot apart. At the end of the month, prepare gherkin cucumbers for pickling. Sow in the naked ground. Sow sweet marjoram and annual aromatic plants including sweet basil.

This is the season when the housekeeper begins to prepare for distilling. Plants are in their fullest perfection when they have grown to their height and are budding for flower. Some of them will be just in that condition at this season, particularly rosemary. Those that are cut now she uses to distil and any remaining bundles are preserved for drying. Hang them in small bundles in an airy garret on lines stretched from wall to wall. Other flowers to be gathered are borage and bugloss.

Look over the espaliers. Thin the wall-fruit. Apricots will hang in vast clusters and peaches grow together in lumps. They are carefully to be thinned. It is better to have a small number well ripened, large and truly flavoured, than a heap of ill-tasted and half-starved ones. The vines must be carefully looked after. Such shoots as have fruits above them must be stopped at the third joint above the bunch, and the others that are for next year's bearing are to be encouraged in the growth. Let the borders around the fruit trees be kept clear of weeds.

June

Sow a second crop of broccoli. If the weather be not too hot and dry, sow turnips in a shady place. They will very soon grow for the table. A crop of French beans and all kinds of lettuce should be sown also at this time. This is a good time for the planting out of those sweet herbs which have been sown for the use of the kitchen. Cabbage and savoy plants sown in the early months will now be fit for planting out. They can be planted between peas and beans and other early crops which will shade them till they have taken root. The early endive will also be ready for transplanting. They will be quickly fit for blanching. Plant out cardoons for the last time. It should stand in a bed of rich and light mould, each plant four foot from another. As it grows, the earth should be carefully hoed up to cover the stalks for blanching. When cardoons are not well blanched they look dirty and eat coarse.

Keep trees well weeded. Go over the fruit trees with a careful eye. Whenever the fruit stands too thick, thin it again. Where the fruit on the wall trees is too exposed to the sun, draw over some leaves by way of a covering. Whenever there happens a shower this month, be sure to visit the wall fruit and look carefully after snails; as also mornings and evenings. New planted trees must have some water at times and mulch should be laid about their roots. All side shoots and ill-placed branches of vines should be removed. Clear away the leaves from the bunches to give them all the advantages of ripening.

July

The products of the spring sowing are now many of them in their perfection, but the gardener should remember, while he is gathering one crop, to make preparation for another: there is the winter to come, in which the products of the kitchen garden are always very desirable and there is also a consideration to be had for the succeeding spring, for there is no time better than this for sowing many of the useful crops that are to come in very early.

Winter spinach is to be sown this month, and onions for the spring. Carrots sowed at this time and kept clear of weeds will also come in very well in spring: and coleworts [kale] and turnips may be sown now with great advantage. Late cauliflowers should now be planted out: and all of the cabbage kind intended for use early in spring. Endive is a herb so very useful by its continuance when others are gone that there always should be fresh sowings of it so long as the season calls for it. This is a very good season for sowing broccoli for the spring. At this time it will be proper to sow French beans and such as are sown now will bear till the very coming on of winter.

Celery and endive are now to be planted out for blanching. The celery is to be blanched by earthing up and the endive by tying it. The great care in drawing the earth up to the celery must be not to bury the head; and a proper time should be taken for tying up the endive; the middle of a dry day is the proper time, for if it be in wet weather, or even when there is a heavy dew, they will rot instead of blanching. Let it be a constant care to water those things which have been transplanted, for otherwise in these dry times they will come to little. Onions will show they now begin to be fit for pulling by the leaves fading. The same will be seen in the shallots and other plants of that kind. They must be laid in an airy room, spread at a distance upon the floor and upon shelves, that they may be thoroughly dried on the outside and may have a sufficient quantity of their juices gone from within to prepare them for keeping.

If asparagus beds have been made in the spring or young artichokes planted, this is the time for preparing and finishing them up. The asparagus beds must be carefully looked over and where any roots have failed the loss must be supplied by new ones. As to artichokes, great care must be taken that they be clear from weeds and the ground well dug about them. The lettuces sown last month will be fit for planting out and they must be watered for three or four evenings after. For these and for the repairing of the asparagus beds, there must be chosen a dripping day. We may assist the deficiencies of nature by artificial waterings: they do not answer like the real and proper drops from heaven: *Set Wet* is an everlasting good rule.

Many seeds will now be ripening, and they must be watched and gathered in due time. They must be gathered on a dry day and dried on a floor in an airy, shady place, after which they must be got out of the heads and pods, and put up for use.

The preceding month was a very favourable time for the budding of fruit trees but this will not be amiss, therefore let such as have omitted it entirely begin now. Cut suckers from the roots of young trees.

After every shower it will be proper to walk the rounds among the fruit trees to look after snails. They will now be seen crawling abroad and much good fruit may be saved by destroying them. Snails are not the only devourers of fine fruit, wasps will eat into it and even so contemptible an insect as the ant will be vastly mischievous. The way to guard against these is to tempt them from the fruit with something they like better; for this purpose let little gallipots of coarse sugar and water be stuck in the forks of trees and wide-mouthed bottles of the same syrup tied to the branches; they will be decoyed into these and the fruit will escape.

August

This is the time of providing for the winter and the following spring. Spinach must be sown and it will grow up for use in the season when most wanted. Onions may be sown also now, but they will be in danger if the winter proves hard. Cabbages that are to stand the winter should be sown about the second week in this month. Cauliflower should be sown a little later but they must be preserved with a great deal of care in winter in frames or under great shelter. Celery sown in preceding months will now be fit for transplanting in order to blanch; and endive will be in the same condition.

September

Few gardeners will have any great opinion of September sowings, yet there are some things to be done in that way very advantageous. Everyone concerned in providing for a table knows the value of spring carrots; the earlier they are brought in the greater is their value and this is one of those things that should be attempted by sowing in September. The chance of hard weather is against them but this is a risk the gardener must run who would take the advantage of the first season. For this purpose choose a well sheltered and warm bed. Sow beans and peas twice. If they escape the severity of winter they will yield very early crops. Taking the two opportunities a fortnight apart one of the two, if not both, may succeed. Sow also young salading and lettuce for the family. Cabbage lettuces are hardiest, but the cos the most valued. Sow mixed seed, let them take their chance together. Cover some with glass. Plant out the last sowing of broccoli and of cauliflower. The coleworts, lettuces and endive sown in July should also be transplanted. The cardoons that were planted out in June will be ready for earthing up in September. On a dry day tie up the leaves with string. Earth each plant up but take care not to bury the heart for then it will decay. Celery that was planted out early should also be earthed up at this time.

October

This is the time for transplanting many of those useful crops which are to stand through the winter and to preserve several others which the cold nights and frosts that are coming on will destroy. Look over your seedling lettuces and plant them out according to their coming in season. Some must be planted in the open ground and some under frames or on beds that may be sheltered from the frost. Dress your asparagus beds and plant cabbage and savoys in between the rows. The method to follow is this: cut down all the weeds on the beds and pile them up to one side. Dig a small trench between the rows of asparagus and bury the weeds at the bottom, replace the soil mixed with a little dung. Plant the cabbage and savoys on that. Earth up cardoons and finachia [*fennel bulbs*] and celery. Earth up the stalks of broccoli plants for it will defend them from frosts. Transplant cauliflower to sheltered spots where they can be covered with bell or hand glasses. Plant out the late-sown cabbage and coleworts. Cut down artichoke plants and trench the ground between the rows and throw the earth up from the trenches over the plants themselves. Put into the open trenches a mixture of two-thirds rotted dung and two-thirds coal ashes.

Prepare borders for new fruit trees. If the earth is too heavy, lighten it with sand and ashes. If it is too light, mix in some clay. Dig in compost. Prune apples, pears and plums. Gather in fruit that is to be kept for the winter. Winter pears should be laid up in heaps in a dry airy store room for a week. They will mellow and grow a little damp by lying together and this will prepare them for standing the rest of the season. They must be carefully wiped one by one; when this is done, they are to be laid upon shelves at such a distance as to be out of the reach of spoiling one another.

Plant gooseberries and currants. Prune currant bushes and work the soil around them. Harvest grapes on dry days. The best way of preserving the grapes is to cut off a joint of the vine with each bunch and to hang them up on strings or lines set a great distance from one another in a room where there is commonly a fire. They will thus keep very good a great part of the winter, and with right management may be preserved through the whole season. Towards the end of the month the vines may be pruned; there is no time fitter, because they will not lose their juices. Weed the strawberry beds, spread compost and rotted dung between the plants.

November

Frosts become severe and crack the earth about the stems of the plants; this lays the roots bare and a continuance of the same weather utterly destroys them. One method is universal against this disaster, which is the earthing up of their stalks.

The use of reed fences is very well known [*for protection against frost and wind*] and they never can be too much recommended. Where there are not a sufficient quantity of them, let others be procured and let them be well secured by tying to poles fast down into the ground. We have named also the use of furze bushes by way of defence against frost. The way of using these is by sticking them into the ground at different distances among the crop, and let them be of such a height as is sufficient for sheltering the growth and the more bushy the better.

Choose a warm border under a hedge or wall on a day when the earth is free from frost. Dig and work it well to a good depth to sow radishes and carrots to come in early. The chance of their succeeding or not depends entirely upon the weather [*but now we have plastic cloches*]. Sow young salading, peas and beans on hot-beds with a moderate degree of warmth. Take up potatoes and lay them by for the service of the kitchen. Where the quantity is considerable, choose a high, airy piece of ground where the soil is naturally dry. Dig a drench three foot deep and two foot and a half broad, and let the length be according to the quantity of potatoes to be preserved. Spread some dry, clean straw over the bottom of the trench and let it rise a little up the sides. Wipe the potatoes clean and lay them two days on the floor of an airy room, then fill the trench with them. Reserve a good quantity for the service of the family so long as they can be expected to keep good. Lay a covering of more clean straw upon the potatoes in the trench and pile over it a ridge of the earth that was dug out in the making of it. The ridge of earth is sufficient to defend them from frosts but may admit wet in a dripping winter. It should be covered with thatch.

Long and deep-rooting plants such as carrots, parsnips, beets, and Dutch parsley [*Hamburg parsley*] should be taken out of the ground, not only for their preservation, but because in continued hard frosts there will be no getting at them. The best method of preserving them is this: spread a large quantity of sand upon the floor that it may dry thoroughly. Take up these roots and wipe the earth clean from them. Lay them separate on a dry floor, from eleven to four o'clock some dry day and then taking them up, wipe them again and lay them separately upon a bed of dry sand. Cover them with more and thus have them for the winter. They will retain their true flavour at all times provided no wet be permitted to come at them.

Where there is an old and entirely useless tree in the orchard it should now be grubbed up without loss of time and a young one planted in its place. The business of pruning wall-trees may now be very well done, taking advantage of mild weather; and it is a work that should not be deferred much longer because the wounds do not heal well when weather is very severe. The several kinds of stone fruit, and the apples and pears, all admit the same time of pruning; but it is best to do the stone fruit first to be sure of a better season, their wounds not healing so easily as those of the others.

The winter pruning of the vine is a very peculiar article of the gardener's business. The hope of a good growth of fruit the succeeding year depends wholly upon this. Consider how quick a grower the vine is and keep that always in mind when pruning. Cut away with boldness and leave but few of the last year's branches. Those which are left must be the largest and the thickest. The smaller must all be taken away.

December

This is a dead season of the year for gardening; the winter crops are all in the ground and those to be sown in spring must not be put in for a considerable time. This would lead many to suppose there was nothing to be done in the garden at the present period and it is accordingly a custom with many who keep a gardener during the summer to discharge him at the approach of this season.

Look to the peas and beans sown late in autumn. Raise a couple of reed hedges at the ends of their bed and scatter some long, dry straw over them to protect against wind and frost. Get out the pods and plants of seeds and remove the seeds clean out of them, put up each in a paper with its proper name and lay them in readiness for sowing. Continue to blanch endives for following the last crop.

Mulch the newly planted fruit trees and stake any rocked by the wind. Cut away in a sloping manner, close to the trunk or stem, any irregular straggling branches, or dead wood, of older trees. Take care to leave the surface smooth otherwise the rains will get in and rot the tree. If you see any particular danger of this, lay over a coarse cloth with some wax and rosin, or a piece of sheet lead.

Cut any quickset hedges and mend any that are defective by cutting a good, stout shoot three parts through and laying it down a little sloping to thicken the bottom of the hedge, which is the most essential part.

Chapter 10

HOW TO USE THE CALENDAR IN FARM AND GARDEN

> When you cut down elm, pine, walnut and all other timber, cut it when the moon is waning, in the afternoon, and not under a south wind.
>
> Cato, *On Farming*.

From its first edition in 1980, *Planting by the Moon* has claimed that the star-zodiac was the framework that really worked. This claim grew out of the belief, that two cycles, the sidereal four-element cycle and the waxing-waning phase cycle of the Moon, were vitally relevant for growing crops and for the rearing of farm animals. The calendar did not use the ascending-descending 'tropical' cycle of the Moon. Readers who were also Bio-Dynamic farmers found this different emphasis on lunar cycles at first difficult to support as they have long been used to taking into account the ascending-descending tropical cycle. This is indeed the underlying principle of all Bio-Dynamic lunar calendars, although there appears little by way of published evidence that it works, and Rudolf Steiner himself made no allusion to it in his original lectures on agriculture. On the contrary, he strongly emphasized the Moon-phase cycle, though this latter is hardly used in Bio-Dynamic calendars – a paradox.

A calendar should not be too complex. Bio-Dynamic calendars tend to display at once five monthly cycles and planetary aspects, which is a lot for the novice reader to absorb. However, we have seen how there exist only two monthly cycles for which there is substantial evidence of important effects on cultivating fruit and vegetables and rearing livestock. Others used in the present calendar, for example the lunar node and perigee which we suggest as no-planting days, have had comparatively little work done on them.

Originally, *Planting by the Moon* did not recommend sowing according to lunar phase, despite the fact that in various parts of Britain and Europe beliefs of this nature can be found which go back several hundred years. These folk-beliefs may have become garbled over the centuries and a new start, a rethinking of the situation, is necessary. It would be hard to find even sugges-tive evidence that planting potatoes during the waning Moon, for example, improves their growth. Would any of the popular almanacs which give this advice to their gardening readers care to produce some evidence in support?

Readers may be inspired to try for themselves sowing one half of a crop at a recommended optimal time and the other half at a negative time, to see whether there is any difference. A proper experiment requires a dozen rows or more, as discussed in Chapter 4. Measured amounts of seed are sown equally in each row, on different days, then final yields per row are compared after each row has been grown for the same length of time, i.e. they are harvested in rotation. Then, over the years, one distinguishes astronomical-lunar rhythms present in the data from differences due to weather and so forth.

Putting together a lunar-gardening calendar and advocating that organic farmers and growers should adjust their work-schedules to fit into it is not done lightly. It does not mean that one is confident of knowing the answers, but more that one has an idea as to what are the right questions. Once in 18.6 years the lunar nodes revolve once round the zodiac and this period has gone by since the first edition of *Planting by the Moon* appeared: a node-cycle. Over this period the author has reached a clearer understanding of the fundamental principles involved ('the silver axioms') and of what evidence supports them. The millenium-synthesis edition you are now reading has one startling difference from the 1980s version: by advocating sowing crops at moonrise it is in effect using the waxing-Moon half of the cycle.

Organizing one's Schedule

The farmer is a busy man, especially in the growing season, and may have little choice when to do things. Beans have to be picked as they ripen, and corn may have to be harvested at the first dry spell. But even if he cannot in practice wait for the Moon it surely adds deeper interest and dignity to his craft to realise that these rhythms do exist and that, for example, the sensible and practical people of ancient Rome used them as a matter of course. Do apples keep better if picked at the New Moon and do tomatoes ripen quicker if picked at the Full? If a farmer can weave these cosmic rhythms into his programme then his productivity is sure to benefit.

So, in deciding when to sow, a farmer has to weigh, on the one hand, soil condition and prevailing weather and, on the other hand, the primary cosmic rhythms which affect his plants. For maximum yields he should sow at the peak times of the sidereal energy cycle involved. Yet there is no point in doing so if the ground is too wet, too dry or too cold. A balance or compromise has to be struck. Much of the farmer's craft involves such judgements.

As more people turn towards life-styles of ecological balance and self-sufficiency, so the demand must surely increase for natural methods of crop improvement which work in harmony with the universe of which we are a part. In this manual we have attempted to bring together the evidence so that the reader can make up his or her own mind upon this old, hardy perennial belief, that the Moon influences the growth and yield of crops.

The paragraphs which follow give some hints on how to use the calendar to best effect, and lay down certain broad principles which can be applied to each day or lunar circumstance.

The Calendar

The calendar of 1999 follows the same principles and layout as that published through the 1980s, plus one or two new features. One hopes the reader will appreciate these fairly novel features, as well as the sense of being linked with millennia of past tradition by using the star-zodiac of antiquity.

The Zodiac Rhythm

For sowing crops observe the four-element cycle. In the calendar these are shown as root, leaf, flower, and fruit or seed days. The table below gives some examples of what these include.

On Root-Days, sow carrots, onions, radishes & potato.

On Leaf-Days, sow cabbages, celery, spinach & lettuce.

On Flower-Days, sow cauliflower, artichoke, broccoli & all flowers.

On Fruit-Seed-days, sow cucumber, corn, peas, beans & tomatoes.

If convenient, sowings are best made on the day nearest to the middle of any of the three Moon-signs of the appropriate element. Soil should be tilled on the day of such a sowing rather than before. Avoid sowing just before the Moon moves out of a sign. Such transition times are given to the nearest hour.

In Australia, one of the fathers of Bio-Dynamics, Alex Podolinsky (whose work is described in *Secrets of the Soil* by Bird & Tompkins) advocates sowing just as the Moon enters a new Moon-sign-element, so the seed has a full two days in that quality before it changes, on the grounds that it takes that long to germinate. That view may be important in drought-prone countries.

From a practical point of view it may be objected that, in the busy schedule of a farmer, it is very difficult to organize sowing activities so that resources are available every nine days or so to sow one particular type of crop. If this is the case, it is important and usually possible to note and avoid the worst days for sowing in any given lunar cycle, even if one cannot make use of the optimal time. By referring to Figure 19 which follows it can be seen that the cycle of four elements follows a regular wave pattern. For example, root crops should be sown during Earth-days for optimal yield. However, if this is impossible, one should at least avoid planting on days at the trough in the cycle when the Moon is in the opposite element, in this case Water-days. This inverse approach can be applied to each of the other elements; for example, Fire-days are the worst times to sow flower crops, which are related to Air-days. By checking the calendar in advance one can see which are the worst days as well as which are the best for planting a particular crop.

Bio-Dynamic farmers believe that any disturbance of the soil should be carried out in the same Moon-sign element in which the seed was sown. Lettuce, for example, is sown on a Leaf-day, so its soil preparation as well as subsequent thinning out, weeding and so forth should also be done on a Leaf-day to enhance the effect. This is something for the reader to mull over.

Potatoes, Carrots and Onions

For root crops to be stored over winter, harvest on a Root-day nearest to the New Moon. In previous editions, we have simply advised that it is best to harvest at New Moon if the crop is destined for storage. Since then, Maria Thun's investigations have found that harvesting as well as sowing can use the element-trigons, i.e. the four types of 'day', and Bio-Dynamic farmers seem to have confirmed this by experience.

For many gardening operations, at least in Britain, one just has to go ahead when weather permits. One can seldom wait a week to harvest corn, once it is ready, as this fact can undermine the practice of using a lunar calenar. But the harvesting of root-crops is an exception. There is no hurry in harvesting the carrots, so one has the option of selecting an optimal time.

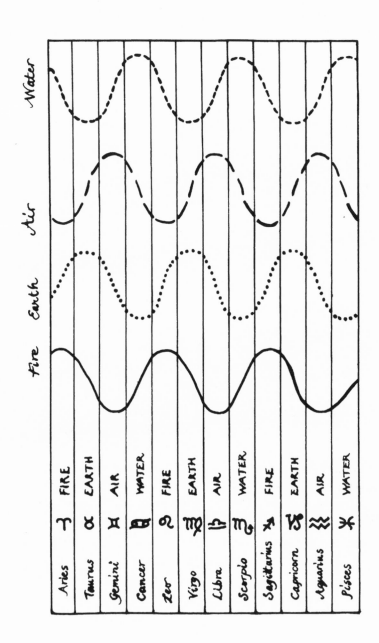

Figure 19. The four-element energy cycles.

Flowers and Venus

For Flower-days, the aspects between the Moon and Venus are given. A Moon-Venus energy is ideal for sowing or planting flowers, especially roses. Roses are ruled by Venus, that is to say, the rose *expresses the being* of Venus. The square aspects are also included, though some might view them as unsuitable, as expressing difficulty and stress; or, alternatively, they could be viewed as assisting the development of structure so readers here have a choice.

Harmony of a Sun-Moon Trine

The calendar gives the trine (120°) angle between Sun and Moon, as happens twice monthly. This is a harmonious aspect free of stress or conflict, and its moment of linking the two luminaries is a good time for many things. Visualize it as a moment of harmony. Like the event of moonrise, it seems never before to have featured in a UK lunar gardening guide: the idea came from the American book *Gardening Success with Lunar Aspects* by Adele Barger (1976). She said that angels helped her with her book so perhaps they deserve the credit! This aspect is of particular interest for crops ruled by the Sun, for example oranges or vines.

Trees & Perennials

When working with plants that become woody or are veritable trees, seek a Saturn aspect for the most propitious time. The calendar gives three types of Moon-Saturn aspect each month: the opposition (180°), the trine (120°) and the sextile (60°). Growers should be mainly concerned with the Saturn aspects on fruit-days as most of their trees and bushes will be fruit-bearing. Because these plants are going to last for years there is all the more reason to identify the optimal date for planting. However, there are perennials that may be influenced by more than one factor. If you are planting a honeysuckle or clematis to grow up one's back wall seek a flower-day and then the calendar gives a choice: a Saturn aspect for durability or a Venus aspect for pretty flowers.

Cow Power

British cows have been mistreated. To help them recover, it is recommended to harness the power of the star Aldebaran, the Bull's Eye. This star has a rose-pink colour and is the very brightest in the Zodiac. It is in the middle of the Taurus constellation and plumb-centre of the sidereal sign of Taurus. The Chaldeans named this constellation 'The Great Bull of Heaven' and their pictograph only included its head, shoulders and long horns.

The Sun reaches Aldebaran on 31st May 1999, and Venus reaches it on 20 April, both of which are therefore days when the farmer can do something positive about his cows. Admittedly, this is not a usual component of the urban allotment or back garden. The conjunction of Venus and Aldebaran is especially propitious for the mating of cows. The Moon meets the star every month and this date can be computed from the calendar as the mid-point of the Moon's path through Taurus, for example on 20th March it conjuncts Aldebaran at 16:00 GMT. Farmers permit cow mating to go on through much of the year and so there will be an opportunity during each month to draw down the power of this particular star. All celestial aspects happening in Taurus are significant for bull- and cow- related events.

Moonrise

The calendar gives the daily event of moonrise, an hour either side being recommended as the best time of the day to undertake any planned planting, sowing or gardening that may be linked to the particular element-sign then in place. As a celestial aspect defines the optimal day so does moonrise, the hour.

In Britain, moonrise happens in the daytime during the waxing phase. The Calendar also gives night-time risings, not just for the benefit of insomniacs, but for persons in other time zones. The event of moonrise is given to within ten minutes. This event would be especially significant if some relevant aspect were being formed by the Moon that day, for example with the Sun or Saturn.

One may wish to sow at moonrise, i.e. in the waxing Moon phase, and just before Full Moon, that is in late afternoon. On the day of Full Moon, the Moon rises as the Sun sets, which might be rather late, so a day or two earlier could be preferable.

Moonrise times are given for zero longitude. For any other longitude, obtain the time of rising (GMT) by adding one hour per fifteen degrees of longitude due west. A user in Bristol, for example, which is three degrees due west, adds ten minutes to the times given in the calendar. There is also a latitude effect, whereby the Moon rises earlier due north, which readers in other latitudes can check by watching it rise and comparing the time of day to that given here.

Fish a-jumpin'

American almanacs give the best times for fishing each day as moonrise and the moment it culminates, that is it reaches its highest point in the sky. This last time can be obtained approximately from the calendar by adding six hours to your local moonrise. Some readers will recall the researches of the American biologist Frank Brown which demonstrated (in the laboratory) that the greatest

JANUARY

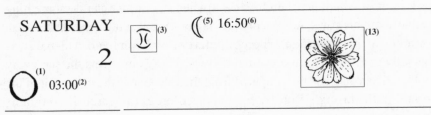

SATURDAY **2**

$\bigcirc$ (1) 03:00(2)

🜊(3)   ☾(5) 16:50(6)   (13)

MARCH

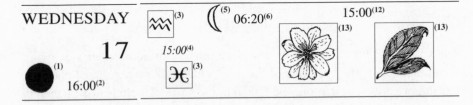

WEDNESDAY **17**

● (1) 16:00(2)

♒(3) 15:00(4) ♓(3)

☾(5) 06:20(6)   15:00(12) (13) (13)

NOVEMBER

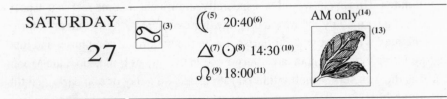

SATURDAY **27**

♌(3)   ☾(5) 20:40(6)

△(7) ☉(8) 14:30(10)

☊(9) 18:00(11)

AM only(14)   (13)

Figure 20. Examples of calendar entries.

(1) Symbol of Moon phase.
(2) Time of New or Full Moon.
(3) Sidereal Moon sign.
(4) Hour of transition from one sign to another.
(5) Symbol indicating moonrise.
(6) Hour of moonrise.
(7) Trine symbol.
(8) Sun symbol (i.e. this is a Sun-Moon trine).
(9) Symbol for the Moon reaching its north node.
(10) Hour of the Sun-Moon trine.
(11) Hour of the Moon's crossing its north Node.
(12) Hour of transition from one element-sign to another.
(13) Symbols indicating which element-sign(s) is(are) in force that day.
(14) General advice about hours of work in a specific element-sign.

metabolic rate in both plants and small animals was registered at the time of moonrise and culmination. The notion of fish being more active at these times is merely a practical illustration of his findings.

The Course of the Day

Gardeners are familiar with the idea that the time of day at which certain operations are performed is important. Planting-out of crops is in general best done in the evening so that they will have the night to settle in and rest. But pruning is best done in the morning so the Sun will dry up the cut surface, thereby inhibiting bleeding.

For effective lunar planting, seed should really begin to germinate as soon as it is sown by immediately beginning to absorb moisture from the soil. For this reason it is preferable, at least in warm weather, to sow seeds in the afternoons so the soil will remain moist for longer after sowing.

Traditionally, one harvested crops in the morning and sowed seeds in the afternoon. One would graft in spring and prune in late autumn and winter. It is likewise recommended that pruning should be done on the waning Moon, grafting on the waxing Moon. Planting-out should be done in the waxing Moon; if possible, in the same element in which the sowings were made.

How to Read the Calendar

Opposite are some sample days from the 1999 calendar, showing what will then be happening in the sky. On the left is given the lunar cycle data and, on the right, the recommended type of plant best sown that day. All times are given in GMT and in the 24-hour form. Aspects and moonrise times are given to the nearest ten minutes, other times to the nearest hour.

JANUARY 2: this is a Flower-day, because the Moon is in Gemini, an Air-constellation. Each day, the ruling sign is denoted by the zodiacal glyph on the left of the entry. Each of the Moon's quarters is shown. This day is a Full Moon, its time to the nearest hour (GMT) is noted next to the sign. Moonrise times are always given next to the sign of a crescent moon at the top of each day's entry. Here it is 4.50 pm (correct to the nearest ten minutes).

MARCH 17: the 'ingress', that is the transition from one sign to another, occurs in the afternoon at 3pm. As the Moon progresses through the zodiac, so the ruling elements shift according to the same timetable. Hence, the morning was in Aquarius, an Air sign, which means working with flowering plants and the afternoon (after 3 pm) is in Pisces, a Water sign, which is the element which

Figure 21. Symbols and glyphs used in the calendar.

●	New Moon (and time)	◐	Full Moon (and time)
◑	Waxing Moon, first quarter	◐	Waning Moon, third quarter
☉	Sun	♈	Aries (Fire)
♀	Venus	♉	Taurus (Earth)
☽	Hour of moonrise	♊	Gemini (Air)
A	Apogee	♋	Cancer (Water)
P	Perigee	♌	Leo (Fire)
☊	North node	♍	Virgo (Earth)
☋	South node	♎	Libra (Air)
☌	Conjunction (aspect 0°)	♏	Scorpio (Water)
✳	Sextile (aspect 60°)	♐	Sagittarius (Fire)
□	Square (aspect 90°)	♑	Capricorn (Earth)
△	Trine (aspect (120°)	♒	Aquarius (Air)
☍	Opposition (aspect 180°)	♓	Pisces (Water)

Flower (Air) element sign

Root (Earth) element sign

Leaf (Water) element sign

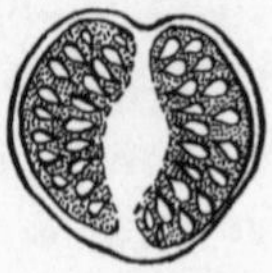

Fruit/seed (Fire) element sign

rules leaf plants. The transition from one sort of plant to another is recorded on the right of the entry. New Moon occurs at 4 pm.

NOVEMBER 27: this day, the Moon is in Cancer, a Water sign, which means that once more leafy plants are the subject of main attention. However, work is only recommended in the morning because the Moon reaches its north node at 6 pm, which means that the day is not recommended for sowing or planting crops. The calendar also records the occurence of a Sun-Moon aspect of trine (120°) in the afternoon at 2.30 pm. All these aspects, mainly Moon-Saturn ones, but also some Sun-Moon and some aspects of the Moon with Venus, together with the crossing of the nodes, and the apogee and perigee of the Moon's circuit of the earth are recorded in this place in the calendar whenever they occur. Their significance or importance to the gardener and farmer has already been discussed in the preceding text and readers should refer to my comments in their proper place to draw any lessons from them. Generally, where it is felt that working in the garden is a bad idea, the fact is noted.

On the right-hand page of the calendar there is space for readers' notes and planting memoranda and there is a short commentary on the lunar and astronomical information expressed by symbols on the facing page. I hope that this may make the calendar easier to use for those who are unfamiliar with the whole concept. Notice, too, that the zodiacal glyphs are identified at the bottom of each calendar page.

The attentive reader needs to have absorbed some of the earlier comments on the possible significance of various astronomical combinations but a bare summary of recommendations would go along the following lines:

Annual crops: follow the four-element rhythms, sowing as near to the centre of the relevant sign as is convenient to you. The same element-sign (Leaf, Root, Fruit, Flower) reappears every nine days, so if you miss the appropriate period the next may still be convenient.

Perennial crops, shrubs or trees: try to take advantage of a Saturn-Moon aspect when planting – these are the most common aspects noted in the calendar; aspects of the Moon and the Sun and the Moon and Venus are less frequently recorded and are always distinguished by their identifying glyphs. If a tree or bush is fruit-bearing try also to plant or graft it on a fruit-day.

The waxing and waning Moon is relevant to diverse gardening and farming activities from grafting and transplanting during a waxing Moon to pruning and gelding livestock during its wane.

The hour of moonrise: this is an important moment in the gardening day, particularly with a view to obtaining maximum yields. Try to sow and plant as close to the hour noted on each day (with adjustments to your longitude and latitude) whenever convenient.

The nodes and perigee: avoid critical times in these cycles. Maria Thun claims to have found that seed quality is impaired in crops sown near the nodes. Bio-Dynamic farmers also avoid sowing at perigee. Our limited experience with these cycles supports the view that planting at such times – including **eclipses** – is best avoided. At the two nodes there may be forces involved which are not beneficial to crops and, in general, sowing at least several hours either side of the Moon's nodes is not recommended.

The ascending/descending Moon: referred to in US almanacs as the Moon riding high or riding low is sometimes considered important. Bio-Dynamic farmers use the concept but we remain unconvinced that it has any relevance.

Pruning: the lunar water-uptake cycle is here relevant and near Full Moon is not recommended for pruning. As Pliny wrote 'All cutting, gathering and trimming is done with less injury to the trees and plants when the Moon is waning than when it is waxing.'

Harvesting: here the old rule recorded by Pliny applies. Fruits to be preserved are best picked at New Moon since these will store better whereas fruits to be eaten fresh are best picked at Full Moon. Crops should be harvested in the same Moon-sign element in which they were sown if the rquirement is to obtain seeds for next year's crop.

Full Moon: where drought is a problem the tendency of seeds to absorb the greatest amount of water on the days prior to the Full Moon should be noted. In dry regions sowing at this time could well lead to optimal germination. Many people swear by sowing crops just before the Full of the Moon but one should not rely on this as improving crop yield.

APPENDIX
Calculating Times

All times given in this book are Greenwich Mean Time. As far as British Summer Time is concerned, between the relevant dates in March and October, British users will have to add one hour to the given times. Users in other parts of the world will need to adjust the times according to the time zone their country adopts with respect to GMT. Such time-zone differences for North America and Australasia are given below.

Time Zone Adjustments for North America

Atlantic	-4 hours
Eastern	-5 hours
Central	-6 hours
Mountain	-7 hours
Pacific	-8 hours
Yukon	-9 hours
Alaska-Hawaii	-10 hours
Bering	-11 hours

Time Zone Adjustments for Australasia

Western Australia	+8 hours
South Australia	+9 $\frac{1}{2}$ hours
Northern Territory	+9 $\frac{1}{2}$ hours
New South Wales	+10 hours
Victoria	+10 hours
Queensland	+10 hours
Tasmania	+10 hours
New Zealand	+12 hours

REFERENCES AND FURTHER READING

1. Abele, U., PhD thesis, U. of Giessen, Germany, 1973.
2. ——, 'Saatzeitversuche mit Radies', *Lebendige Erde* 6 223–5, 1975.
3. Abrami, G., 'Correlations between Lunar Phases and Rhythmicities in Plant Growth under Field Conditions', *Canadian Journal of Botany,* 1972, No. 50, 2157–2166.
4. Andrews, E., 'Moon Talk, the Cyclic Periodicity of Postoperative Hemorrhage', *Journal of Florida Medical Assocn.,* May 1960, 1362–66.
5. Baker, M., *Gardener's Magic and Folklore,* Universe, New York, 1978.
6. Barger, A., *Gardening Success with Lunar Aspects,* 1977, AFA US.
7. Beeson, C., 'The Moon and Plant Growth', *Nature,* 1946, 158, 572–3.
8. Bell, B. & Defouw, R., 'Concerning a Lunar modulation of Geomagnetic Activity' *Journal Geophysical Research* 1964, 69, 3169–3174.
9. ——, 'Dependence of the Lunar Modulation of Geomagnetic Activity on the Celestial Latitude of the Moon', *Journal Geophysical Research,* 1966, 71, 3, 951–957.
10. Best, S., 'Lunar Influence in Plant Growth: A Review of the Evidence', *Phenomena,* 2.3–2.4, August 1978.
11. *Biodynamics: New Directions for Farming and Gardening in New Zealand,* Random Century N.Z., 1989.
12. Bishop, C., 'Moon Influences in Lettuce Growth', *Astrological Journal,* 10, No. 1, Winter 77/78.
13. Bose, J. C., *Plant Response as a Means of Physiological Investigation,* Longmans, London, 1906.
14. Bradley, D., Woodbury, M., and Brier, G., 'Lunar Synodical Period and Widespread Precipitation', *Science,* 137, 1962, 748–9 (also Adderley, E. & Bowen, E., Ibid, 749–50).
15. Brier, G. & Bradley, D., 'Lunar Synodic Precipitation in the United States', *Journal Atmos. Sci.,* 1964, 21, 386–395.
16. Brown, F., 'The Rhythmic Nature of Animals and Plants', *Cycles,* April, 1960, 81–92.
17. ——, & Chow, C., 'Lunar-correlated Variations in Water Uptake by Bean Seeds', *Biological Bulletin,* Oct., 1973, 145, 265–278.
18. Burns, J.T., *Cosmic Influences on Humans, Animals and Plants, An Annotated Bibliography,* Magill (US), 1997.
19. Burr, H. S., 'Diurnal Potentials in the Maple Tree', *Yale Journal of Biology & Medicine,* 1945, 17, 727–734.
20. ——, *The Fields of Life: Our Links with the Universe,* NY, 1973.
21. Carpenter, T. *et al.,* 'Observed Relationship between lunar tidal cycles and formation of hurricanes and tropical storms', *Monthly Weather Review,* 1972, 100, 451–6.
22. Culpeper, N., *Complete Herbal,* Foulsham, London.
23. Currie, R. 'Evidence for 18.6-year signal in Temperature and Drought conditions in North America since AD 1800', *Journal of Geophysical Research,* 1981, 86, 11055.
24. ——, 'Examples & Implications of 18.6- and 11-yr Terms in World Weather Records', in *Climate,* Ed. Rampino *et al.,* NY, 1987.
25. Cutler, W., 'Lunar and Menstrual Phase Locking', *American Journal of Obstetric Gynecology,* 1980, 137, 834.
26. ——, *et al.,* 'Lunar influences on the reproductive cycle in women', *Human Biology,* 1987, 59, 959–72.
27. *Dariotus Redivivus, or a brief introduction to the judgement of the stars,* 1653 (agricultural section by Nathaniel Spark).

28. Dewey, E. & Mandino, O., *Cycles–the mysterious forces that trigger events*, New York, 1973.
29. Dixon, B., 'Plant Sensations', *Omni,* Dec., 1978, 24.
30. Domin, A., ed., *Organic Wholefoods, Naturally Delicious Cuisine,* Konemann, 1997.
31. Dubrov, A., *The Geomagnetic Field and Life* (trans. from Russian), 1978.
32. ——, *Human Biorhythms and the Moon*, Nova Science, NY, 1996, 117.
33. Elliott, J., *Plants & Planets*, Astrological Gardening, 1996.
34. *Elm Farm Research Centre Bulletin*, April 1995 (Info. on Organic Farming)
35. Estienne, C., & Liebault, J., *La Maison Rustique*, trans. Surfleet, 1616.
36. Fagan, C., *Zodiacs Old and New,* Anscombe and Co., London, 1951.
37. Farbridge K. & Leatherland, J., 'Lunar Periodicity of Growth Cycles in Rainbow Trout', *Journal of Interdisciplinary Cycles Research*, 1987, 18, 169–177.
38. Farrar, J., 'Sunspot Weather', *Farmers Weekly,* Feb. 28, 1975.
39. Field, J., 'A Lutheran Astrologer: Johannes Kepler', *Arch. Hist. Exact Sci.* 1984, 31, 190–268 (has his calendar predictions for 1602).
40. Graf, U., PhD thesis. Zurich E.T.H., 1977.
41. Grau, G. *et al.*, 'Lunar Phasing of the Thyroxine Surge', *Science,* 1981, 211, 607–9.
42. Graviou, E., 'Analogies between Rhythms in Plant Material in Atmospheric Pressure and Solar-Lunar Periodicities', *International Journal of Biometeorology,* 1978, Vol. 22, No. 2.
43. Hesiod, *The Homeric Hymns and Homerica,* trans. H.G. Evelyn-White, 1977.
44. Hill, T., *The Gardener's Labyrinth*, 1577, OUP, 1987.
45. Joly, N., *Le Vin du Ciel à la Terre*, Paris, 1997.
46. Kerr, A. & Marshall,C., 'Planting by the Moon', *Harvests* [Journal of N.Z. Bio-Dynamic Assoc.], Summer 1997.
47. Kerr, R. A, 'Fickle Sun could be altering Earth's Climate after all', *Science*, 269, Aug. 1995, 633.
48. King, J., 'Solar Radiation Changes and the Weather', *Nature,* 245, Oct., 1973, 443–446.
49. ——, *et al.,* 'Agriculture and Sunspots', *Nature,* 252, Nov 1, 1974, 2–3.
50. Kokus, M., 'The 18.6-year Cycle in Drought and Flood: A Review of the Climate Research of Robert Currie', *Cycles,* Aug 1988,189–191,
51. Kolisko, L., *The Moon and the Growth of Plants,* Anthroposophical Press, London, 1938, 1975 (1933, in German).
52. ——, *Agriculture of Tomorrow*, 1939, 1982.
53. Kollerstrom, N., 'Zodiac Rhythms in Plant Growth – Potatoes', *Mercury Star Journal*, Summer 1977.
54. ——, 'Plant Response to the Synodic Lunar Cycle: A Review', *Cycles,* 31, 1980, 61–63.
55. ——, 'A Lunar Sidereal Rhythm in Crop Yield', *Correlation,* Jun 81, 1, 44–53.
56. ——, 'Testing the Lunar Calendar' *Biodynamics* 185 (US), Winter 1993, 44–48.
57. ——, 'The Star-Zodiac of Antiquity', *Culture and Cosmos,* Winter 1997, 5–22.
58. Knight, J. 'Moon Up – Moon Down: the story of the Solunar Theory', *Biodynamics* (US), 1972.
59. Lai, T. M., 'Phosphorus and Potassium Uptake by Plants Relating to Moon Phases', *Biodynamics* (US), Summer, 1976.
60. Lampkin, N. *Organic Farming,* 1990.
61. Lethbridge, M., 'Relationship between thunderstorm frequency and lunar phase', *Journal of Geophysical Research,* 1970, 75, 5153.
62. Lieber, A. L., *The Lunar Effect,* Corgi, 1979.
63. Lücke, J., *Untersuchungen...* PhD, U. of Giessen 1982, 71, 74.
64. Mather, M., 'The Effect of Temperature and the Moon on Seedling Growth', *Journal of the Royal Horticultural Society,* 1942, 67, 264–270.
65. Markham, G., *The Whole Art of Husbandry,* 1631 (trans. of a continental work, originally published in the 1570s).

66. Maw, M. G., 'Periodicities in the Influences of Air Ions on the Growth of Garden Cress, *Lepidium Sativum* L.', *Canadian Journal of Plant Science,* 1967, 47, 499–505.

67 Messegu , M., *Of Men and Plants*, NY, 1972, 9.

68. McClintock, M., 'Menstrual Synchrony and Suppression', *Nature,* 1971, 229, 244–5.

69. Oehmke, M.G., 'Lunar Periodicity in Flight Activity of Honey Bees', *Journal of Interdisciplinary Cycles Research,* 1973, 4, 319–335.

70. Panzer, J. J., 'Lunar Correlated Variations in Water Uptake and Germination in 3 Species of Seeds', PhD, U. of Tulane, 1976.

71. Playfair, G. & Hill, S., *The Cycles of Heaven,* Pan Books, 1979.

72. Pliny, *History of Nature,* Vol. 18, Section 75 (Loeb Classics, 1961).

73. Podolinsky, A. *Bio-Dynamic Agriculture Introductory Lectures,* Vol. 1, Australia 1990.

74. Powell, R. and Treadgold, P., *The Sidereal Zodiac,* Anthroposophical Publications, 1979.

75. Rossignol M. *et al.,* 'Lunar Cycle and Nuclear DNA variations in Potato callus', *Geocosmic Relations* (Ed Tomassen, Pudoc, Netherlands 1990), 116–126.

76. Rounds, H. D., 'A semi-lunar periodicity of neurotransmitter-like substances from plants', *Physiologia Plantarium,* 1982.

77. Sattler, F. & Wistinghausen E., *Bio-Dynamic Farming Practice*, CUP 1989.

78 Spiess, H., 'Chronobiological Investigations...', *BAH,* 1990, 7, 165–89.

79. ——, *Biologische Rhythmen im Landbau,* 3 vols., Darmstadt 1994.

80. Steiner, R. *Agriculture,* 1938, 1993 (US).

81. ——, *Health & Illness,* Anthropological Press NY, 1983 edition.

82. Stolov, H. & Cameron A., 'Variation of Geomagnetic Activity with Lunar Phase'm, *Journal Geophysical Research,* 1964, 69, 4975–4982.

83. Taverner, E., 'The Roman Farmer and the Moon', *Transactions & Proceedings of the American Philological Association,* 1918, 49, 67–82.

84. Temple, J., *Gardening Without Chemicals,* 1986.

85. ——, 'Checking the value of planting by the zodiac', *Here's Health,* November 1982, 144–5.

86. Theroux, M., 'Lunar Influence on ... Colloidal Silver', *Borderlands, A Quarterly Journal of Borderlands Research* (US), 1997, 3, 52–4.

87. Thompson, L., 'The 18.6-year and 9.3-year Lunar cycles Their Possible Relation to Agriculture', *Cycles,* Dec. 1988, 286–7.

88. ——, 'The 18.6-year Lunar cycle: Its possible Relation to Agriculture', *Cycles,* March 1989, 65–9.

89. Thun, M., 'Nine Years Observation of Cosmic Influences on Annual Plants', *Star and Furrow,* 22, Spring 1964.

90. ——, & Heinze, H., *Mondrhythmen im Siderischen Umlauf und Pflanzenwachstum,* Darmstadt, 1979.

91. ——, *Work on the Land & the Constellations*, Lanthorn Press, East Grinstead, 1991.

92. ——, *Milch und Milchverarbeitung,* 1992.

93. Timmins, C., *Planting by the Moon,* Aries Press, Chicago, 1939.

94. Treloar A., *et al.,* 'Variations of the Human Menstrual Cycle through Reproductive Life', *International Journal of Fertility,* 1967, 12, 77–126.

95. *New Scientist,* 19 March, 1981, 740, 'US Study shows that back to Nature Farming makes sense'.

96. Vines, R. G., 'Possible Relationships between Rainfall, Crop Yields and the Sunspot Cycle', *Journal of the Australian Institute of Agricultural Science,* March/June, 1977, 3–13.

97. Vollman, F., 'The Menstrual Cycle', *Major Problems in Obstetrics & Gynecology,* Philadelphia, Vol 7, 1977, 54–56.

98 Walker, C., ed., *Astronomy Before the Telescope* , 1996, Ch. 3: 'Astronomy & Astrology in Mesopotamia'.

PLANTING
BY THE
MOON

1999

JANUARY

FRIDAY

1

☿ Gemini ☽ 15:50

✳ 03:00

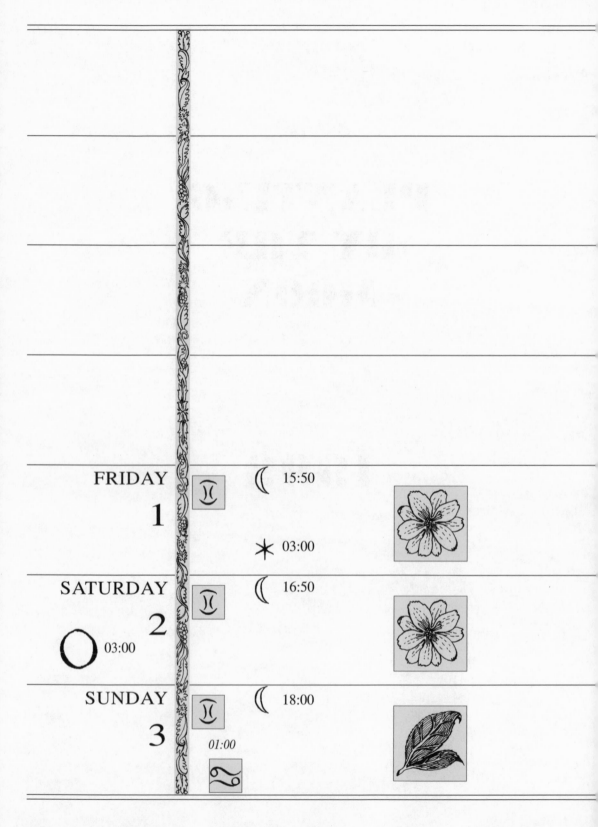

SATURDAY

2

○ 03:00

☿ Gemini ☽ 16:50

SUNDAY

3

☿ Gemini ☽ 18:00

01:00

♋ Cancer

JANUARY

The Moon is in the harmonious sextile aspect with Saturn early this morning. A good time to be working with trees and perennials.

FRIDAY

1

Full Moon, an optimal time for water absorption and germination. For most impressive results, work from 16:00 to 18:00, around the time of moonrise.

SATURDAY

2

The shift from Gemini to Cancer (Air to Water) is in the middle of the night, so the whole day can be devoted to leaf plants, for instance preparing and planting a rhubarb bed.

SUNDAY

3

 Libra
Air

 Scorpio
Water

 Sagittarius
Fire

 Capricorn
Earth

 Aquarius
Air

 Pisces
Water

JANUARY

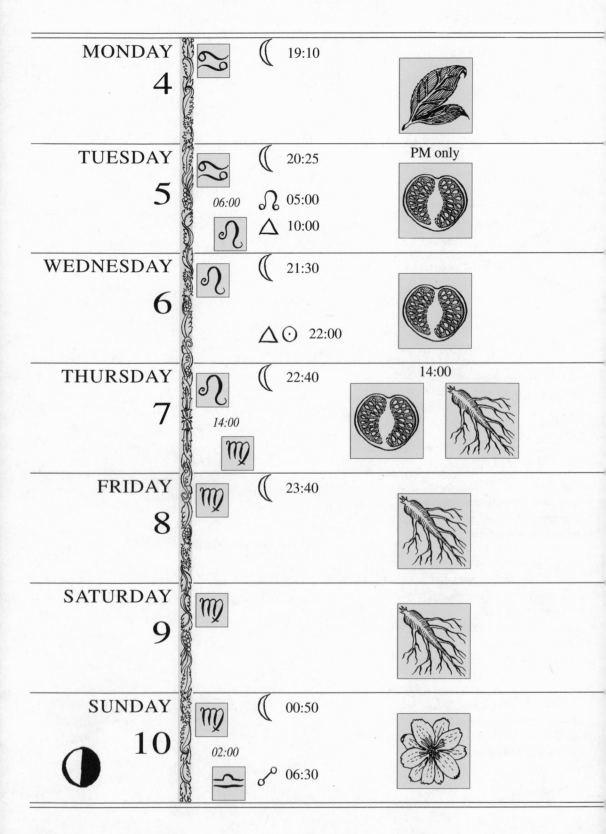

MONDAY **4**	♋	☽ 19:10	
TUESDAY **5**	♋ *06:00* ♌	☽ 20:25 ♌ 05:00 △ 10:00	PM only
WEDNESDAY **6**	♌	☽ 21:30 △ ☉ 22:00	
THURSDAY **7**	♌ *14:00* ♍	☽ 22:40	14:00
FRIDAY **8**	♍	☽ 23:40	
SATURDAY **9**	♍		
SUNDAY **10**	♍ *02:00* ♎	☽ 00:50 ♎ 06:30	

JANUARY

If you have glass or plastic cloches, think about sowing some early salad crops.

The Moon has reached its north node, with is usually a stressful time, but is quickly followed by the trine aspect, which is more harmonious. Work only in the afternoon.

TUESDAY

5

The Sun-Moon trine is a moment particularly free of stress. The afternoon is the most productive time to work with fruit/seed plants.

WEDNESDAY

6

The change from fruit to root element occurs at the hour indicated.

THURSDAY

7

Time perhaps to think of sowing some early radish under glass or other protection.

FRIDAY

8

SATURDAY

9

The Moon is in opposition to Saturn in the early evening. Saturn aspects govern particularly the growth of perennials and trees.

SUNDAY

10

 Libra
Air

 Scorpio
Water

 Sagittarius
Fire

 Capricorn
Earth

 Aquarius
Air

Pisces
Water

JANUARY

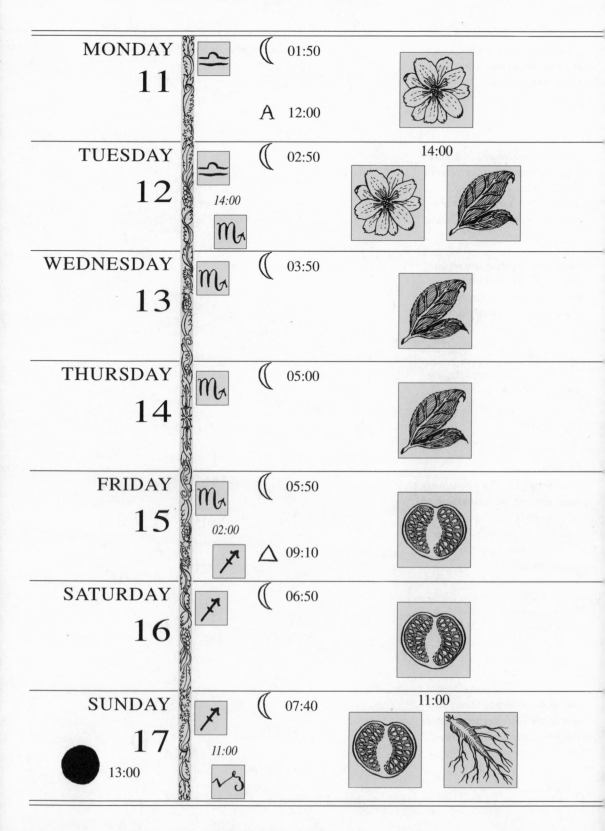

MONDAY **11**	♎ ☾ 01:50 / A 12:00	
TUESDAY **12**	♎ ☾ 02:50 / *14:00* ♏	14:00
WEDNESDAY **13**	♏ ☾ 03:50	
THURSDAY **14**	♏ ☾ 05:00	
FRIDAY **15**	♏ ☾ 05:50 / *02:00* ♐ △ 09:10	
SATURDAY **16**	♐ ☾ 06:50	
SUNDAY **17**	♐ ☾ 07:40 / *11:00* ♑ ● 13:00	11:00

 Aries *Fire*   Taurus *Earth*   Gemini *Air*   Cancer *Water*   Leo *Fire*   Virgo *Earth*

JANUARY

Apogee at midday, a time of imbalance in the moon's influence, best to avoid sowing seed.

MONDAY

11

A change from flower to leaf element in the afternoon.

TUESDAY

12

The Moon being on the wane, it is a good time to think of pruning shrubs and trees.

WEDNESDAY

13

THURSDAY

14

The change from flower to fruit occurs at night, so the whole day can be devoted to the second element. The beneficent trine aspect with Saturn should extends its influence through the day.

FRIDAY

15

Pruning vines, fruit trees and bushes, also treating them with any winter washes.

SATURDAY

16

New moon is at lunchtime, and there is a change from fruit to root element at the end of the morning.

SUNDAY

17

 Libra
Air

 Scorpio
Water

 Sagittarius
Fire

 Capricorn
Earth

 Aquarius
Air

 Pisces
Water

JANUARY

MONDAY **18**	♑	☾ 08:20	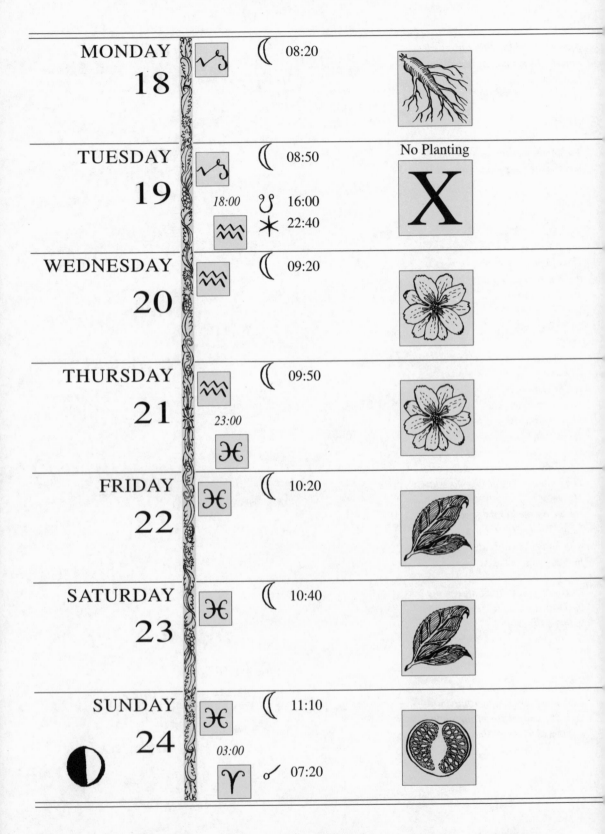
TUESDAY **19**	♑ ~ *18:00* ♒	☾ 08:50 ☊ 16:00 ✳ 22:40	No Planting **X**
WEDNESDAY **20**	♒	☾ 09:20	
THURSDAY **21**	♒ ~ *23:00* ♓	☾ 09:50	
FRIDAY **22**	♓	☾ 10:20	
SATURDAY **23**	♓	☾ 10:40	
SUNDAY **24** ◐	♓ ~ *03:00* ♈	☾ 11:10 ☌ 07:20	

 ♈ Aries *Fire*   ♉ Taurus *Earth*   ♊ Gemini *Air*   ♋ Cancer *Water*   ♌ Leo *Fire*   ♍ Virgo *Earth*

JANUARY

Remember that for best results the ground should be worked during the element sign of its intended crop.	**MONDAY** **18**
The Moon crosses its south node in the afternoon and is in sextile aspect to Saturn much later in the evening.	**TUESDAY** **19**
Thinks of concentrating work into the morning hours to take advtange of Moonrise.	**WEDNESDAY** **20**
The change from flower to leaf element is late in the evening so should not affect the day's plans. Planting or sowing is best done in the middle of each period shown for the appropriate element.	**THURSDAY** **21**
Work is best within one hour of Moonrise.	**FRIDAY** **22**
Work especially hard between the hours of 10:00 and 12:00.	**SATURDAY** **23**
The change of elements occurs again in the middle of the night. The Moon is in (stressful) conjunction with Saturn in the morning.	**SUNDAY** **24**

 Libra
Air

 Scorpio
Water

 Sagittarius
Fire

 Capricorn
Earth

 Aquarius
Air

 Pisces
Water

JANUARY

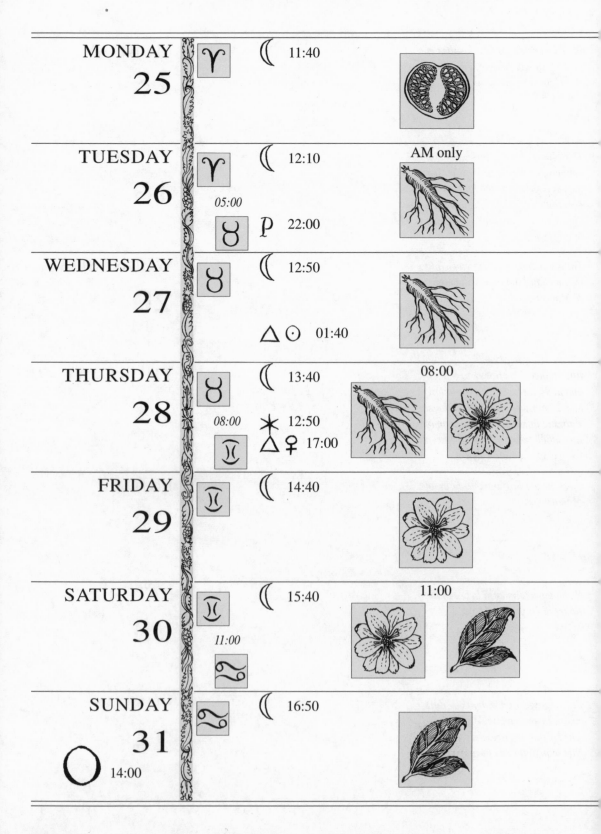

MONDAY 25   ♈   ☾ 11:40

TUESDAY 26   ♈   ☾ 12:10   AM only
05:00   ♉   ♇ 22:00

WEDNESDAY 27   ♉   ☾ 12:50
△ ☉   01:40

THURSDAY 28   ♉   ☾ 13:40   08:00
08:00   ⚹ 12:50
♊   △ ♀ 17:00

FRIDAY 29   ♊   ☾ 14:40

SATURDAY 30   ♊   ☾ 15:40   11:00
11:00   ♌

SUNDAY 31   ♌   ☾ 16:50
◯ 14:00

 Aries *Fire*   Taurus *Earth*   Gemini *Air*   Cancer *Water*   Leo *Fire*   Virgo *Earth*

JANUARY

MONDAY

25

The change in the element sign happens early in the morning, but the occurrence of the perigee is generally reckoned stressful, hence the counsel to suspend operations in the afternoon.

TUESDAY

26

The Moon moves into the trine aspect with the Sun during the night. A very good day for root crop sowings.

WEDNESDAY

27

Both the sextile aspect to Saturn and the trine aspect to Venus are harmonious. An excellent day for working with flowering plants, particularly the hours 13:00–15:00.

THURSDAY

28

Concentrate work within one hour of Moonrise.

FRIDAY

29

A change of elements towards the end of the morning.

SATURDAY

30

Full moon: 'It being near full moon, I cut off my wife's hair,' recorded the 18th-century diarist, Nicholas Blundell of Lancashire.

SUNDAY

31

 Libra
Air

 Scorpio
Water

 Sagittarius
Fire

 Capricorn
Earth

 Aquarius
Air

 Pisces
Water

FEBRUARY

MONDAY 1
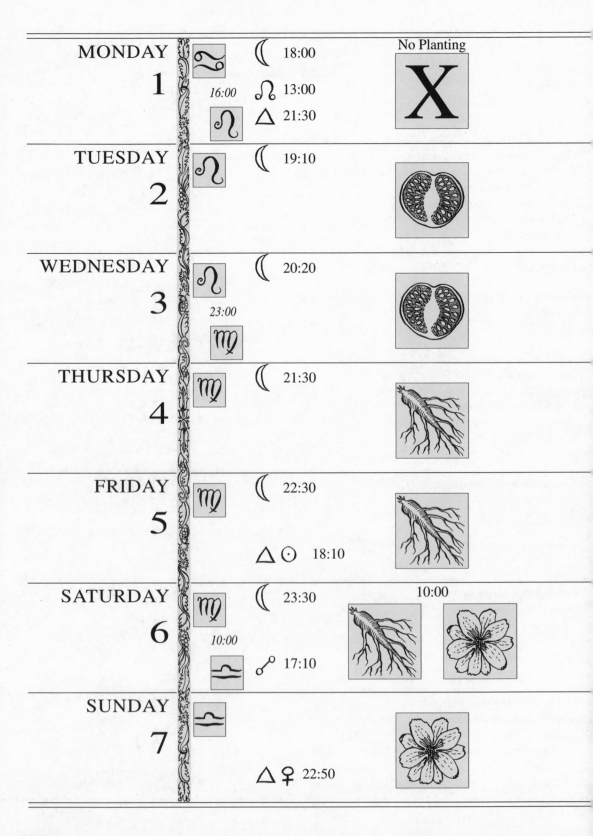
♋ 16:00 ♌
🌙 18:00
♌ 13:00
△ 21:30

No Planting
X

TUESDAY 2
♌
🌙 19:10

WEDNESDAY 3
♌ 23:00 ♍
🌙 20:20

THURSDAY 4
♍
🌙 21:30

FRIDAY 5
♍
🌙 22:30
△ ☉ 18:10

SATURDAY 6
♍ 10:00 ♎
🌙 23:30
⚯ 17:10
10:00

SUNDAY 7
♎
△ ♀ 22:50

 Aries *Fire*   Taurus *Earth*   Gemini *Air*   Cancer *Water*   Leo *Fire*   Virgo *Earth*

FEBRUARY

The moon's crossing through its north node in the middle of the day is reason enough to suspend any planting.

MONDAY

1

TUESDAY

2

WEDNESDAY

3

THURSDAY

4

The Sun/Moon aspect this evening is the harmonious trine (120°).

FRIDAY

5

A change of element-signs in the morning is followed by the Moon and Saturn being in opposition (180°), neither being indicators of calm or fecundity.

SATURDAY

6

The Moon and Venus aspect is at trine (120°) late in the evening.

SUNDAY

7

 Libra
Air

 Scorpio
Water

 Sagittarius
Fire

 Capricorn
Earth

 Aquarius
Air

 Pisces
Water

FEBRUARY

MONDAY 8

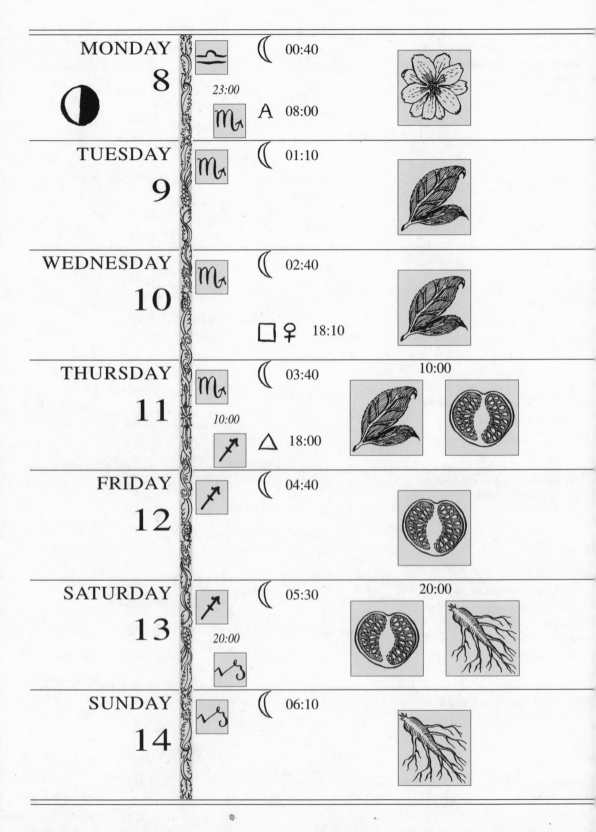

≈ ☾ 00:40

23:00

♏ A 08:00

TUESDAY 9

♏ ☾ 01:10

WEDNESDAY 10

♏ ☾ 02:40

□ ♀ 18:10

THURSDAY 11

♏ ☾ 03:40

10:00

♐ △ 18:00

10:00

FRIDAY 12

♐ ☾ 04:40

SATURDAY 13

♐ ☾ 05:30

20:00

20:00

♑

SUNDAY 14

♑ ☾ 06:10

FEBRUARY

The Moon is at its apogee in the morning, a time of imbalance in geomagnetic forces.

MONDAY

8

TUESDAY

9

The Venus-Moon aspect is square (90°). This relationship is thought mainly relevant to flower cultivation.

WEDNESDAY

10

The Moon-Saturn aspect is trine (good), following a shift in element-signs from leaf to fruit in the morning.

THURSDAY

11

FRIDAY

12

The fire element, governing fruit or seed crops continues to rule through the working day, a shift to the earth element (roots) occurring in the evening.

SATURDAY

13

SUNDAY

14

 Libra
Air

 Scorpio
Water

 Sagittarius
Fire

 Capricorn
Earth

 Aquarius
Air

 Pisces
Water

FEBRUARY

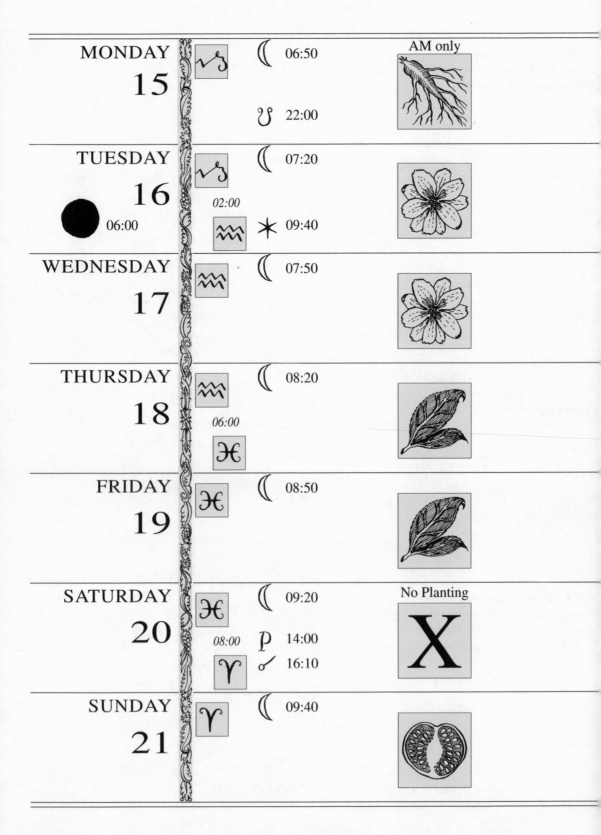

MONDAY 15
♑ ☾ 06:50
☊ 22:00
AM only

TUESDAY 16
● 06:00
♑ ☾ 07:20
02:00
♒ ✳ 09:40

WEDNESDAY 17
♒ ☾ 07:50

THURSDAY 18
♒ ☾ 08:20
06:00
♓

FRIDAY 19
♓ ☾ 08:50

SATURDAY 20
♓ ☾ 09:20
08:00
♈ ♃ 14:00
♂ 16:10
No Planting
X

SUNDAY 21
♈ ☾ 09:40

FEBRUARY

The passage through the south node in the evening makes morning working only advisable.

MONDAY

15

The New Moon, the sextile aspect is also encouraging, and there is a shift from an Earth sign to one favouring flowering plants. Work especially between 07:00 and 10:00.

TUESDAY

16

WEDNESDAY

17

An Air sign gives way to a Water sign (leafy plants) early in the morning.

THURSDAY

18

FRIDAY

19

The perigee and the conjunction indicated both suggest that cultivation is left to one side for the day, allowing general tidying and maintenance work.

SATURDAY

20

SUNDAY

21

 Libra
Air

 Scorpio
Water

 Sagittarius
Fire

 Capricorn
Earth

 Aquarius
Air

 Pisces
Water

FEBRUARY

MONDAY 22

♈ ☽ 10:20 11:00

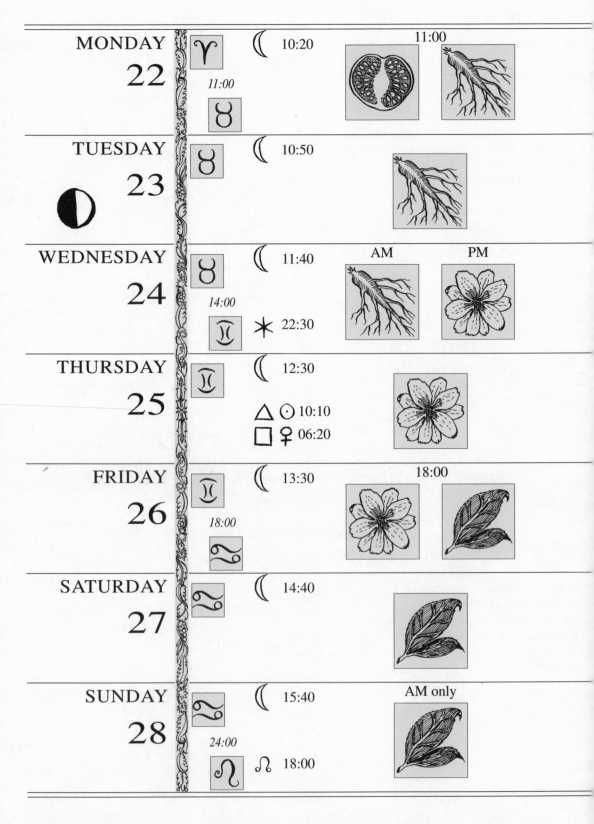

11:00 ♉

TUESDAY 23

♉ ☽ 10:50

WEDNESDAY 24

♉ ☽ 11:40 AM PM

14:00 ♊ ✶ 22:30

THURSDAY 25

♊ ☽ 12:30

△ ☉ 10:10
□ ♀ 06:20

FRIDAY 26

♊ ☽ 13:30 18:00

18:00 ♋

SATURDAY 27

♋ ☽ 14:40

SUNDAY 28

♋ ☽ 15:40 AM only

24:00 ♌ ☊ 18:00

FEBRUARY

The change from fruit or seed to root element happens at mid-morning.

MONDAY

22

The best time for sowing root plants is 10:00 to 12:00.

TUESDAY

23

Divide the day between root and flower elements. The Moon and Saturn form a sextile aspect late in the evening.

WEDNESDAY

24

The Moon-Sun aspect is trine in the morning, whereas the less beneficent square aspect between the Moon and Venus is formed at the end of the day.

THURSDAY

25

The shift from flower to leaf element happens at the end of the working day.

FRIDAY

26

Concentrate work on leaf crops in the hours 14:00–16:00.

SATURDAY

27

The Moon crossing its north node at the end of the afternoon results in the suggestion that cultivation should be restricted to the morning hours.

SUNDAY

28

 Libra
Air

 Scorpio
Water

 Sagittarius
Fire

 Capricorn
Earth

 Aquarius
Air

 Pisces
Water

MARCH

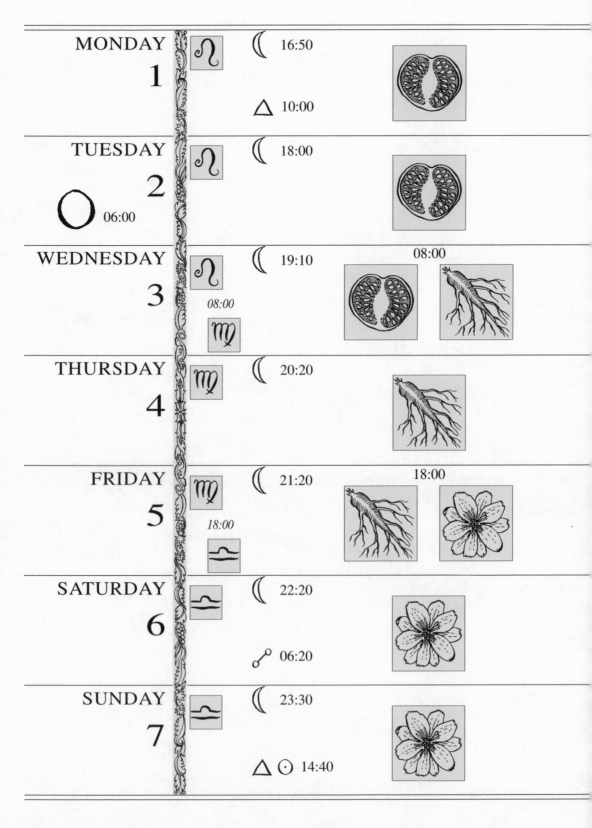

MONDAY 1
♌   ☾ 16:50
△ 10:00

TUESDAY 2
♌   ☾ 18:00
○ 06:00

WEDNESDAY 3
♌   ☾ 19:10
08:00
♍
08:00

THURSDAY 4
♍   ☾ 20:20

FRIDAY 5
♍   ☾ 21:20
18:00
♎
18:00

SATURDAY 6
♎   ☾ 22:20
☍ 06:20

SUNDAY 7
♎   ☾ 23:30
△ ☉ 14:40

 Aries *Fire*   Taurus *Earth*   Gemini *Air*   Cancer *Water*   Leo *Fire*   Virgo *Earth*

MARCH

The Moon and Saturn form a trine aspect in the morning: a good moment to work with fruit trees.	**MONDAY** **1**
Full Moon in the early morning.	**TUESDAY** **2**
A change of element signs from fruit or seed plants to root plants at the beginning of the working day.	**WEDNESDAY** **3**
	THURSDAY **4**
A change of element signs from Earth (root plants) to Air (flowering plants) at the end of the day.	**FRIDAY** **5**
The Moon/Saturn aspect is in opposition (180°) at the beginning of the morning. Think of working particularly with perennials.	**SATURDAY** **6**
The Moon forms a trine aspect with the Sun. A good day in general, especially for flowering plants.	**SUNDAY** **7**

 Libra
Air

 Scorpio
Water

 Sagittarius
Fire

 Capricorn
Earth

 Aquarius
Air

 Pisces
Water

MARCH

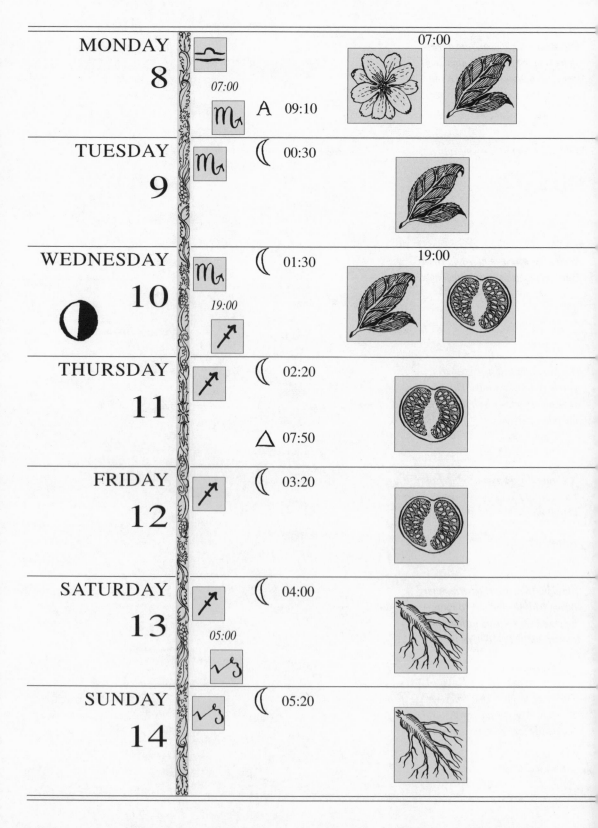

MONDAY 8
♎ 07:00
♏ A 09:10
07:00

TUESDAY 9
♏ ☾ 00:30

WEDNESDAY 10
♏ ☾ 01:30
19:00
♐ 19:00
19:00

THURSDAY 11
♐ ☾ 02:20
△ 07:50

FRIDAY 12
♐ ☾ 03:20

SATURDAY 13
♐ ☾ 04:00
♑ 05:00

SUNDAY 14
♑ ☾ 05:20

MARCH

The Moon is at its apogee at nine o'clock in the morning, this is a time of imbalance. There is a shift in element-signs before breakfast.

MONDAY

8

TUESDAY

9

At the end of the day there is a move from leaf plants to fruit/seed plants.

WEDNESDAY

10

The Moon-Saturn aspect is trine, which is harmonious. Think of working especially with fruit trees and other perennials.

THURSDAY

11

FRIDAY

12

The move from one elent to another – from fruit/seed plants to roots – happens very early in the morning, leaving the whole day to the one type.

SATURDAY

13

SUNDAY

14

 Libra
Air

 Scorpio
Water

 Sagittarius
Fire

 Capricorn
Earth

 Aquarius
Air

 Pisces
Water

MARCH

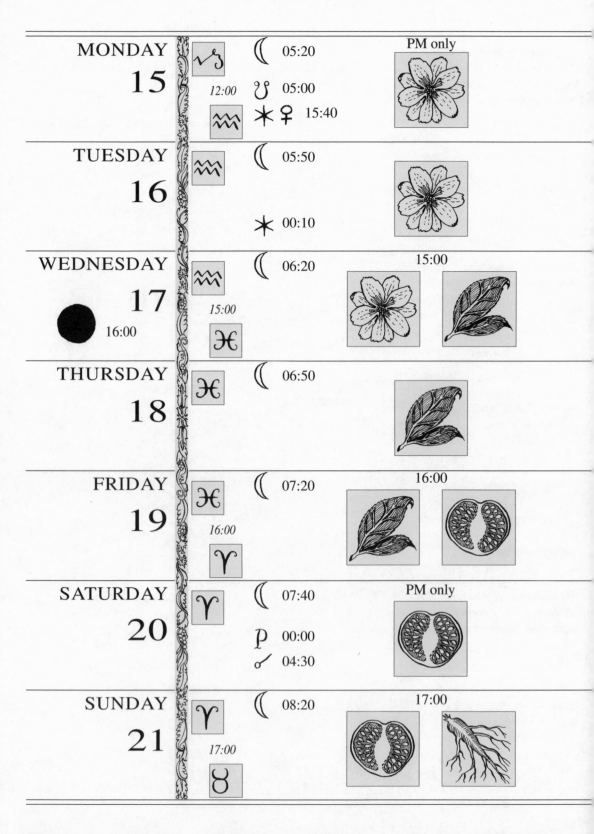

MONDAY 15	♑ 12:00 ♒	☾ 05:20 ☋ 05:00 ✳ ♀ 15:40	PM only	
TUESDAY 16	♒	☾ 05:50 ✳ 00:10		
WEDNESDAY 17 ● 16:00	♒ 15:00 ♓	☾ 06:20	15:00	
THURSDAY 18	♓	☾ 06:50		
FRIDAY 19	♓ 16:00 ♈	☾ 07:20	16:00	
SATURDAY 20	♈	☾ 07:40 ℞ 00:00 ☌ 04:30	PM only	
SUNDAY 21	♈ 17:00 ♉	☾ 08:20	17:00	

 Aries *Fire*   Taurus *Earth*   Gemini *Air*   Cancer *Water*   Leo *Fire*   Virgo *Earth*

MARCH

The passage of the Moon through its south node suggests suspension of gardening in the morning. The sextile aspect of the Moon with Venus is a better harbinger for working with flowers.	**MONDAY** **15**
The Moon forms a sextile aspect to Saturn during the night. Think of working especially with perennials.	**TUESDAY** **16**
New Moon and, later on, a shift from a flowering plant element sign to one governing leaf plants. Planting out is best done during a waxing Moon.	**WEDNESDAY** **17**
	THURSDAY **18**
A change from Water (leaf) to Fire (fruit and seed) element at the end of the afternoon. Try to time planting or sowing to the middle of the appropriate sign period.	**FRIDAY** **19**
Perigee at the very start of the day. Gardening is best restricted to the afternoon. The Moon/Saturn conjunction is also a period of relative stress.	**SATURDAY** **20**
Vernal equinox. A change from fruit or seed to an Earth sign occurs at the end of the afternoon. Moonrise early in the morning would suggest concentrating work in that half of the day.	**SUNDAY** **21**

 Libra
Air

 Scorpio
Water

 Sagittarius
Fire

 Capricorn
Earth

 Aquarius
Air

 Pisces
Water

MARCH

MONDAY 22 ♉ ☾ 08:50

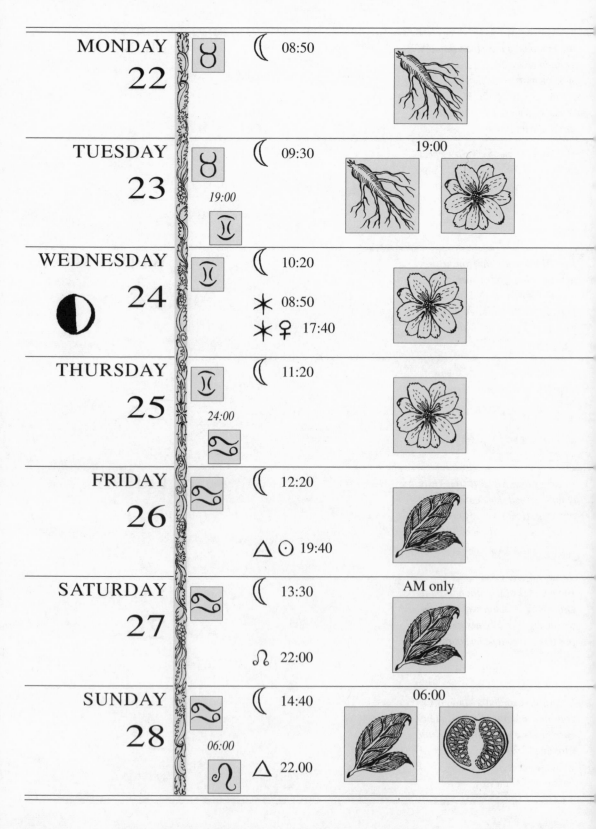

TUESDAY 23 ♉ ☾ 09:30

19:00

♋

19:00

WEDNESDAY 24 ♋ ☾ 10:20

✳ 08:50

✳ ♀ 17:40

THURSDAY 25 ♋ ☾ 11:20

24:00

♋

FRIDAY 26 ♋ ☾ 12:20

△ ☉ 19:40

SATURDAY 27 ♋ ☾ 13:30

AM only

♌ 22:00

SUNDAY 28 ♋ ☾ 14:40

06:00

06:00

♌ △ 22.00

 Aries *Fire*   Taurus *Earth*   Gemini *Air*   Cancer *Water*   Leo *Fire*   Virgo *Earth*

MARCH

<table>
<tr><td>

Work mainly in the morning hours (soon after moonrise).

</td><td>

MONDAY

22

</td></tr>
<tr><td></td><td>

TUESDAY

23

</td></tr>
<tr><td>

The Moon forms a sextile aspect to two planets, Saturn in the morning and Venus in the afternoon. This is a particularly good day to wait for if work with flowering plants is on the agenda.

</td><td>

WEDNESDAY

24

</td></tr>
<tr><td>

The best time to think of work is moonrise and an hour thereafter.

</td><td>

THURSDAY

25

</td></tr>
<tr><td>

The Moon/Sun aspect is trine early in the evening.

</td><td>

FRIDAY

26

</td></tr>
<tr><td>

The passage of the Moon through its north node in the evening is the reason for the advice to restrict planting to the morning hours only.

</td><td>

SATURDAY

27

</td></tr>
<tr><td>

There is a Moon/Saturn trine in the evening, and the element-signs have shifted from Water to Fire early in the morning.

</td><td>

SUNDAY

28

</td></tr>
</table>

 Libra
Air

 Scorpio
Water

 Sagittarius
Fire

 Capricorn
Earth

 Aquarius
Air

 Pisces
Water

MARCH/APRIL

MONDAY 29 ♌ ☾ 15:50

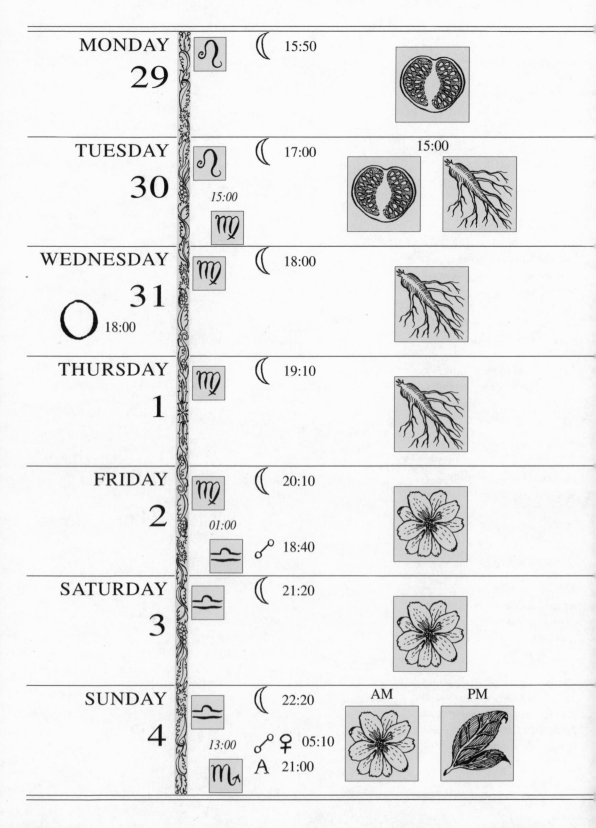

TUESDAY 30 ♌ *15:00* ♍ ☾ 17:00 — 15:00

WEDNESDAY 31 ○ 18:00 ♍ ☾ 18:00

THURSDAY 1 ♍ ☾ 19:10

FRIDAY 2 ♍ *01:00* ♎ ☾ 20:10 — ☌ 18:40

SATURDAY 3 ♎ ☾ 21:20

SUNDAY 4 ♎ *13:00* ♏ ☾ 22:20 — ☌ ♀ 05:10 — A 21:00 — AM — PM

MARCH/APRIL

The best time to think of fruit/seed plant sowings is moonrise and an hour thereafter.

MONDAY

29

A shift from fruit/seed to root plants occurs in the middle of the afternoon.

TUESDAY

30

Full Moon tonight. Consider root plant sowings at the end of the afternoon (just before moonrise).

WEDNESDAY

31

THURSDAY

1

Moon/Saturn form the aspect known as opposition(180°), a time of imbalance.

FRIDAY

2

SATURDAY

3

The Moon is at the apogee of its course round the earth during the evening; the Moon/Venus aspect is in opposition (180°) early in the morning.

SUNDAY

4

 Libra
Air

 Scorpio
Water

 Sagittarius
Fire

 Capricorn
Earth

 Aquarius
Air

 Pisces
Water

APRIL

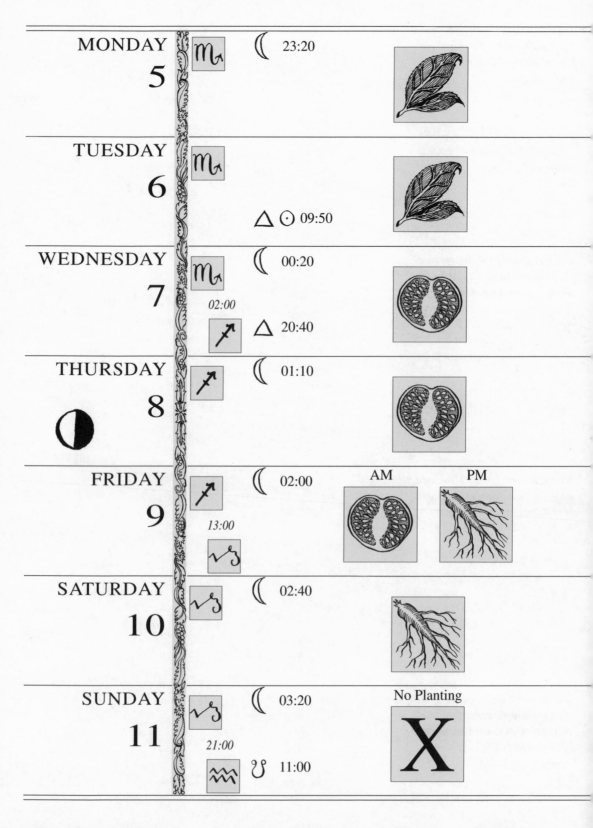

MONDAY 5 ♏ ☾ 23:20

TUESDAY 6 ♏ △ ☉ 09:50

WEDNESDAY 7 ♏ ☾ 00:20
02:00 ♐ △ 20:40

THURSDAY 8 ♐ ☾ 01:10

FRIDAY 9 ♐ ☾ 02:00   AM   PM
13:00 ♑

SATURDAY 10 ♑ ☾ 02:40

SUNDAY 11 ♑ ☾ 03:20   No Planting
21:00 ♒ ☊ 11:00   **X**

♈ Aries *Fire* ♉ Taurus *Earth* ♊ Gemini *Air* ♋ Cancer *Water* ♌ Leo *Fire* ♍ Virgo *Earth*

APRIL

MONDAY 5

TUESDAY 6

The Moon forms a trine aspect with the Sun.

WEDNESDAY 7

The change in element happens in the middle of the night, leaving the whole day for fruit and seed plants. The Moon forms a trine aspect with Saturn in the evening.

THURSDAY 8

FRIDAY 9

Divide the day between fruit and seed plants on the one hand, and root plants on the other.

SATURDAY 10

SUNDAY 11

The Moon's traverse of the south node mid-morning suggests a suspension of planting and sowing activities on this day.

 Libra
Air

 Scorpio
Water

 Sagittarius
Fire

 Capricorn
Earth

 Aquarius
Air

 Pisces
Water

APRIL

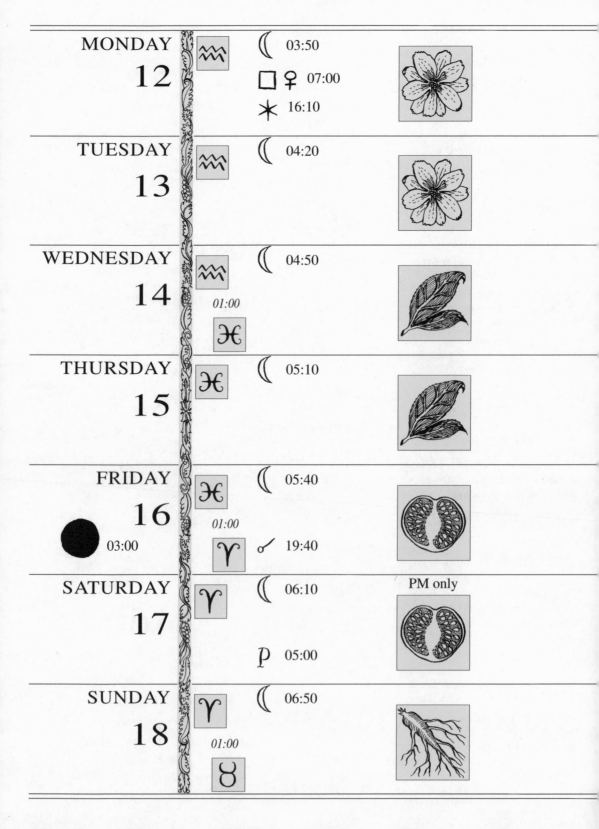

MONDAY 12
♒︎
☽ 03:50
□ ♀ 07:00
✴ 16:10

TUESDAY 13
♒︎
☽ 04:20

WEDNESDAY 14
♒︎
01:00
♓︎
☽ 04:50

THURSDAY 15
♓︎
☽ 05:10

FRIDAY 16
● 03:00
♓︎
01:00
♈︎
☽ 05:40
♂ 19:40

SATURDAY 17
♈︎
☽ 06:10
℞ 05:00
PM only

SUNDAY 18
♈︎
01:00
♉︎
☽ 06:50

APRIL

The Moon's square aspect to Venus early in the morning may affect working with flowering plants; the sextile aspect to Saturn suggests emphasis on perennials.

MONDAY

12

TUESDAY

13

The changes in element signs this week occur at dead of night, leaving the days relatively unaffected.

WEDNESDAY

14

THURSDAY

15

New Moon. The Moon is in conjunction with Saturn (0°) at the beginning of the evening.

FRIDAY

16

The Moon's perigee early in the morning is the cause of the suggestion to restrict cultivation to the afternoon.

SATURDAY

17

SUNDAY

18

 Libra
Air

 Scorpio
Water

 Sagittarius
Fire

 Capricorn
Earth

Aquarius
Air

 Pisces
Water

APRIL

MONDAY 19 — ♉ ☽ 07:30

TUESDAY 20 — ♉ ☽ 08:20
01:00 ♊ ✳ 21:20

WEDNESDAY 21 — ♊ ☽ 09:10

THURSDAY 22 — ♊ ☽ 10:20
04:00 ♋

FRIDAY 23 — ♋ ☽ 11:20
AM only
☊ 23:00

SATURDAY 24 — ♋ ☽ 12:30
11:00
11:00 ♌

SUNDAY 25 — ♌ ☽ 13:40
△ ☉ 06:50
△ 09.10

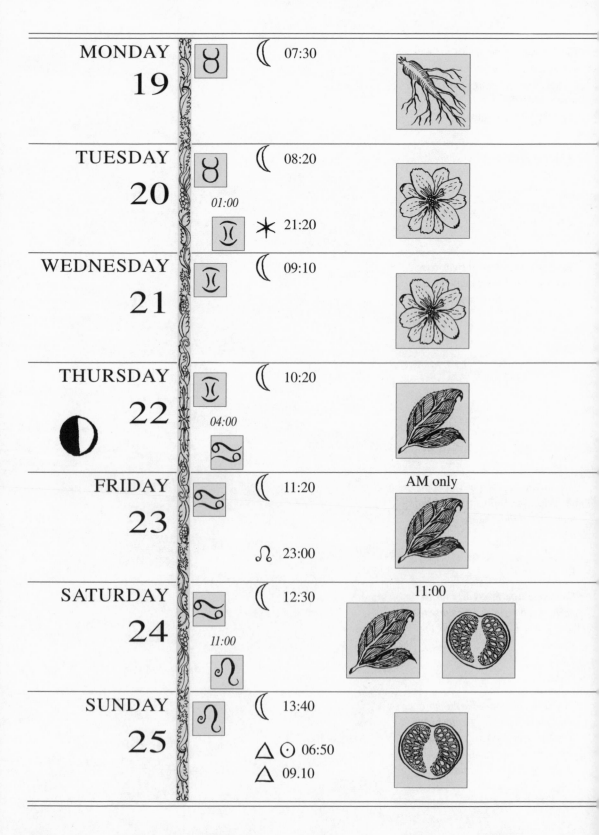

APRIL

MONDAY
19

A change in element-signs happens during the night, and there is a Moon/Saturn sextile aspect formed during the evening.

TUESDAY
20

Take advantage of the daytime moonrise to undertake any sowing or planting at the most propitious moment.

WEDNESDAY
21

THURSDAY
22

The crossing of the north node late in the evening suggests that the morning should be the time for cultivation.

FRIDAY
23

A change from Water to Fire elements happens late in the morning.

SATURDAY
24

Two trines are formed in the morning, one with Saturn, the other with the Sun. This is a very good day for working with perennials and fruit trees, especially vines.

SUNDAY
25

 Libra
Air

 Scorpio
Water

 Sagittarius
Fire

 Capricorn
Earth

 Aquarius
Air

 Pisces
Water

APRIL/MAY

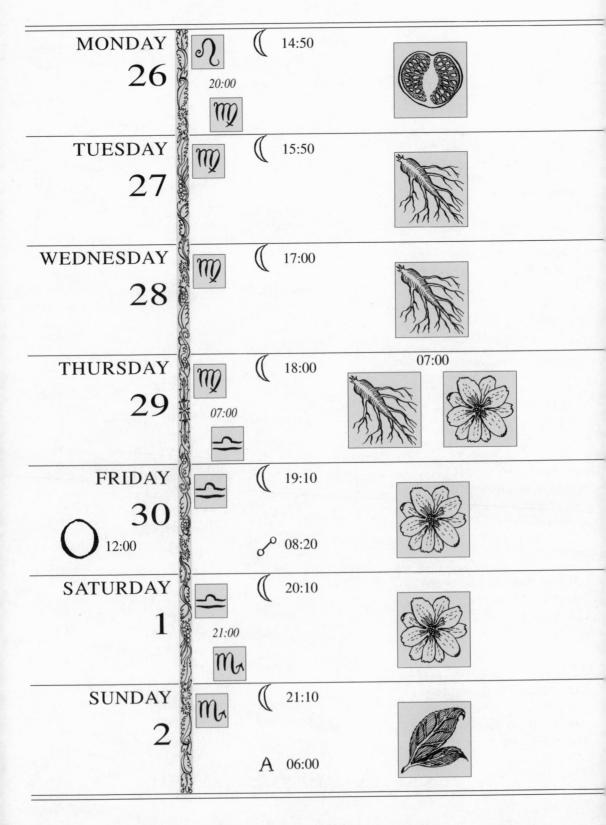

MONDAY 26 ♌ ☾ 14:50 · 20:00 ♍

TUESDAY 27 ♍ ☾ 15:50

WEDNESDAY 28 ♍ ☾ 17:00

THURSDAY 29 ♍ ☾ 18:00 · 07:00 ♎ · 07:00

FRIDAY 30 ♎ ☾ 19:10 · ○ 12:00 · ☊ 08:20

SATURDAY 1 ♎ ☾ 20:10 · 21:00 ♏

SUNDAY 2 ♏ ☾ 21:10 · A 06:00

APRIL/MAY

Moonrise is again during daylight hours – consider it when planning any sowing.

MONDAY

26

TUESDAY

27

Sow roots, particularly at the end of the afternoon.

WEDNESDAY

28

A change of ruling sign from that favouring root crops to flowering plants at the beginning of the working day.

THURSDAY

29

The Moon forms the aspect with Saturn known as opposition (180°). Full Moon, the optimum time for sowing and planting.

FRIDAY

30

A change in elements happens during the evening.

SATURDAY

1

The apogee of the Moon's course round the Earth occurs early in the morning.

SUNDAY

2

 Libra
Air

 Scorpio
Water

 Sagittarius
Fire

 Capricorn
Earth

 Aquarius
Air

 Pisces
Water

MAY

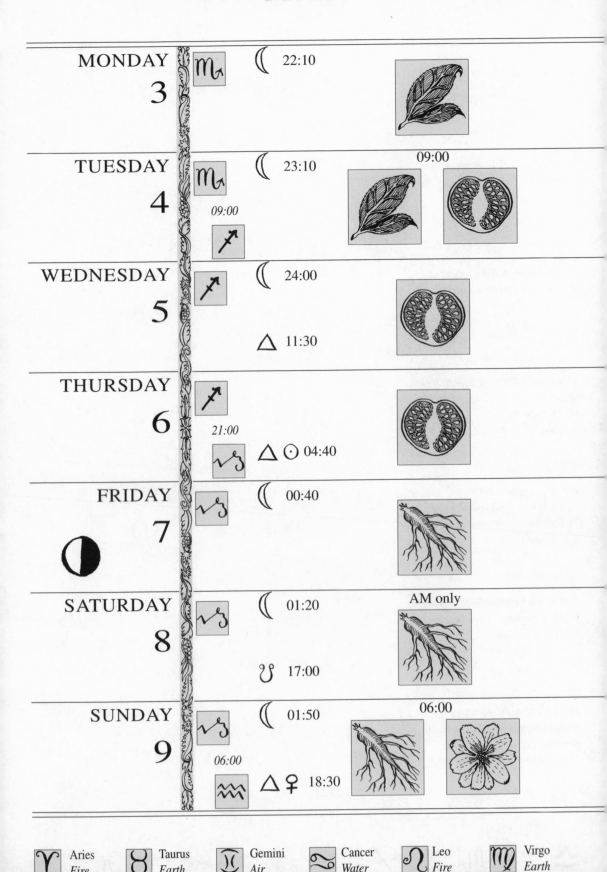

MONDAY **3**	♏	☾ 22:10	
TUESDAY **4**	♏	☾ 23:10	09:00
	09:00 ↗		
WEDNESDAY **5**	↗	☾ 24:00 △ 11:30	
THURSDAY **6**	↗		
	21:00 ♑	△ ☉ 04:40	
FRIDAY **7**	♑	☾ 00:40	
SATURDAY **8**	♑	☾ 01:20 ☊ 17:00	AM only
SUNDAY **9**	♑	☾ 01:50	06:00
	06:00 ♒	△ ♀ 18:30	

♈ Aries *Fire*	♉ Taurus *Earth*	♊ Gemini *Air*	♋ Cancer *Water*	♌ Leo *Fire*	♍ Virgo *Earth*

MAY

MONDAY

3

The change in element happens at the beginning of the working day.

TUESDAY

4

The Moon forms a trine aspect with Saturn in the morning. This is generally a very good day for sowing or planting fruit or seed crops.

WEDNESDAY

5

The Moon/Sun aspect is trine (120°).

THURSDAY

6

FRIDAY

7

The Moon crosses its south node in the afternoon, hence morning work recommended.

SATURDAY

8

There is a Moon/Venus trine aspect at the end of the day: an especially good day for working.

SUNDAY

9

 Libra *Air*   Scorpio *Water*   Sagittarius *Fire*   Capricorn *Earth*   Aquarius *Air* Pisces *Water*

MAY

MONDAY **10**	♒︎	☾ 02:20 ✳ 07:20	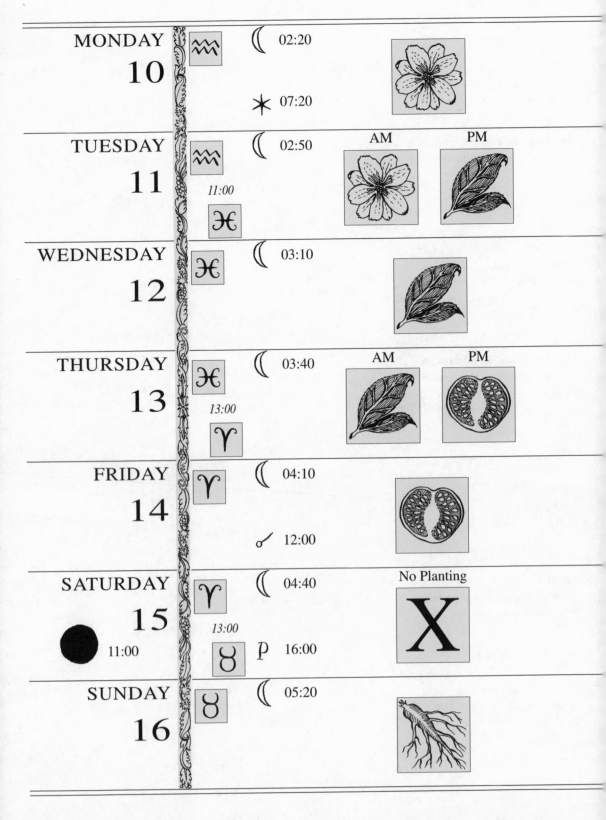	

MONDAY 10 — ♒︎ — ☾ 02:20 — ✳ 07:20

TUESDAY 11 — ♒︎ — ☾ 02:50 — *11:00* ♓︎ — AM / PM

WEDNESDAY 12 — ♓︎ — ☾ 03:10

THURSDAY 13 — ♓︎ — ☾ 03:40 — *13:00* ♈︎ — AM / PM

FRIDAY 14 — ♈︎ — ☾ 04:10 — ♂ 12:00

SATURDAY 15 — ♈︎ — ☾ 04:40 — *13:00* ♉︎ ♃ 16:00 — ● 11:00 — No Planting **X**

SUNDAY 16 — ♉︎ — ☾ 05:20

 ♈ Aries *Fire*   ♉ Taurus *Earth*   ♊ Gemini *Air*   ♋ Cancer *Water*   ♌ Leo *Fire*   ♍ Virgo *Earth*

MAY

The Moon/Saturn aspect is sextile in the morning.	**MONDAY** **10**
The change of elements happens at the end of the morning.	**TUESDAY** **11**
	WEDNESDAY **12**
Again, the change of element occurs conveniently halfway through the day.	**THURSDAY** **13**
The Moon/Saturn aspect is conjunction (0°).	**FRIDAY** **14**
The Moon's orbit is at its perigee, so the recommendation is to suspend planting and sowing. New Moon.	**SATURDAY** **15**
	SUNDAY **16**

 Libra
Air

 Scorpio
Water

 Sagittarius
Fire

 Capricorn
Earth

 Aquarius
Air

 Pisces
Water

MAY

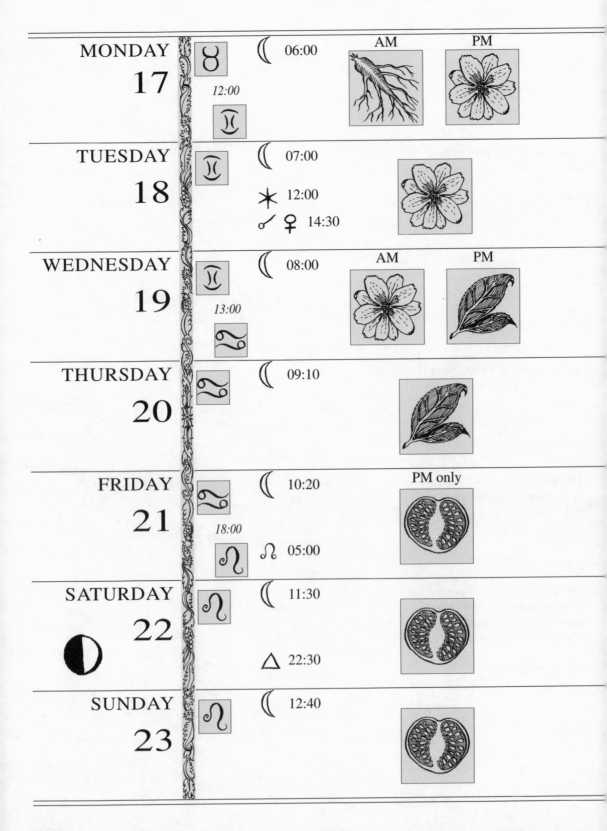

MONDAY 17

☿ (Taurus)
☾ 06:00
12:00
♊ (Gemini)

AM | PM

TUESDAY 18

♊ (Gemini)
☾ 07:00
✳ 12:00
☌ ♀ 14:30

WEDNESDAY 19

♊ (Gemini)
☾ 08:00
13:00
♋ (Cancer)

AM | PM

THURSDAY 20

♋ (Cancer)
☾ 09:10

FRIDAY 21

♋ (Cancer)
☾ 10:20
18:00
♌ (Leo) ♌ 05:00

PM only

SATURDAY 22

♌ (Leo)
☾ 11:30
△ 22:30

SUNDAY 23

♌ (Leo)
☾ 12:40

♈ Aries *Fire*   ♉ Taurus *Earth*   ♊ Gemini *Air*   ♋ Cancer *Water*   ♌ Leo *Fire*   ♍ Virgo *Earth*

MAY

There is a shift from root (Earth) to flower (Air) element at midday.

MONDAY
17

The Moon/Venus aspect is conjunction in the afternoon; it is preceded by a sextile aspect of the Moon with Saturn. This is a brilliant day to work with flowering plants, trees and shrubs.

TUESDAY
18

The element changes from Air (flower) to Water (leaf) around the middle of the day, permitting an equal division of the pattern of work.

WEDNESDAY
19

THURSDAY
20

The passage of the Moon through its north node restricts planting to the afternoon.

FRIDAY
21

The Moon/Saturn aspect is trine, the most benevolent. Work especially on perennials and fruit trees, especially from noon onwards.

SATURDAY
22

SUNDAY
23

 Libra
Air

 Scorpio
Water

 Sagittarius
Fire

 Capricorn
Earth

 Aquarius
Air

 Pisces
Water

MAY

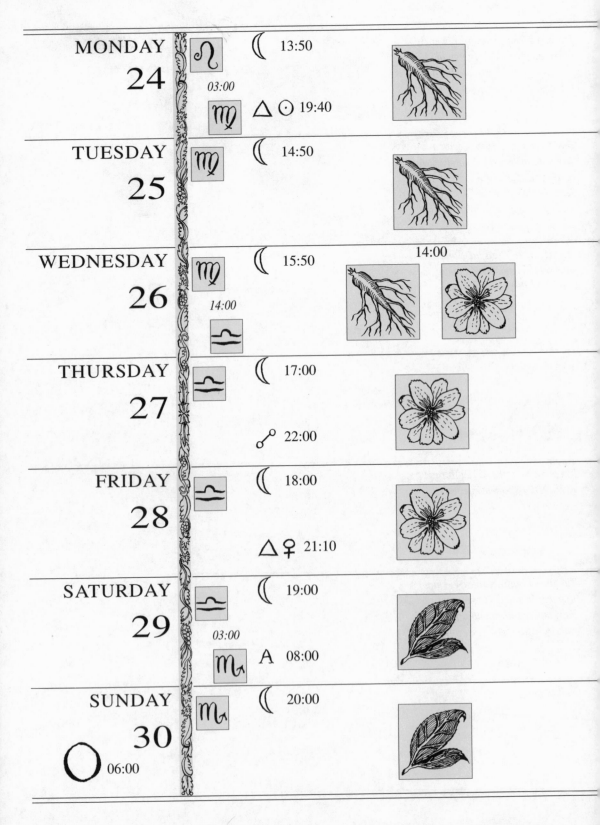

MONDAY 24
♌
03:00
♍ △ ☉ 19:40
☽ 13:50

TUESDAY 25
♍
☽ 14:50

WEDNESDAY 26
♍
14:00
♎
☽ 15:50
14:00

THURSDAY 27
♎
☽ 17:00
☌ 22:00

FRIDAY 28
♎
☽ 18:00
△ ♀ 21:10

SATURDAY 29
♎
03:00
♏ A 08:00
☽ 19:00

SUNDAY 30
♏
☽ 20:00
○ 06:00

 Aries *Fire*   Taurus *Earth*   Gemini *Air*   Cancer *Water*   Leo *Fire*   Virgo *Earth*

MAY

The Moon is trine to the Sun early in the evening. The change in elements occurred in the middle of the night, leaving the whole day for root plants.	**MONDAY** **24**
The best time to work with root crops is between 15:00 and 18:00 today.	**TUESDAY** **25**
A shift from roots to flowering plants in the middle of the day.	**WEDNESDAY** **26**
The Moon forms an oppositional aspect with Saturn. Work with flowering plants especially from the hours of 16:00 to 18:00.	**THURSDAY** **27**
There is a Moon/Venus trine aspect at the end of the evening.	**FRIDAY** **28**
The apogee of the Moon's course round the Earth occurs early in the morning, a time of imbalance.	**SATURDAY** **29**
Full Moon at six in the morning.	**SUNDAY** **30**

 Libra *Air*   Scorpio *Water*   Sagittarius *Fire*   Capricorn *Earth*   Aquarius *Air*   Pisces *Water*

MAY/JUNE

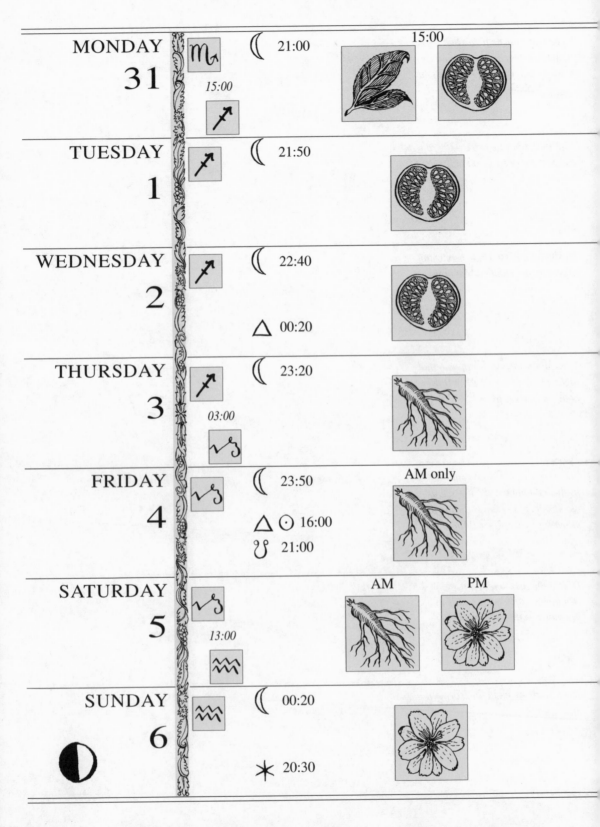

MONDAY 31 — ♍ ☽ 21:00 — 15:00 — ♐ 15:00

TUESDAY 1 — ♐ ☽ 21:50

WEDNESDAY 2 — ♐ ☽ 22:40 — △ 00:20

THURSDAY 3 — ♐ ☽ 23:20 — ♑ 03:00

FRIDAY 4 — ♑ ☽ 23:50 — △ ☉ 16:00 — ☊ 21:00 — AM only

SATURDAY 5 — ♑ 13:00 ♒ — AM — PM

SUNDAY 6 — ♒ ☽ 00:20 — ✳ 20:30

MAY/JUNE

A change from leaf to fruit/seed plants happens in the afternoon.

MONDAY

31

TUESDAY

1

The Moon and Saturn form a trine aspect in the middle of the night.

WEDNESDAY

2

The shift of elements is during the night so the whole day can be devoted to root crops.

THURSDAY

3

The Moon crosses its south node in the evening, hence the recommendation to work only during the morning. There is a Moon/Sun trine aspect in the afternoon.

FRIDAY

4

Divide the day between two types of plants: roots in the morning, flowering plants in the afternoon.

SATURDAY

5

The Moon/Saturn aspect is sextile after dark.

SUNDAY

6

 Libra
Air

 Scorpio
Water

 Sagittarius
Fire

 Capricorn
Earth

 Aquarius
Air

 Pisces
Water

JUNE

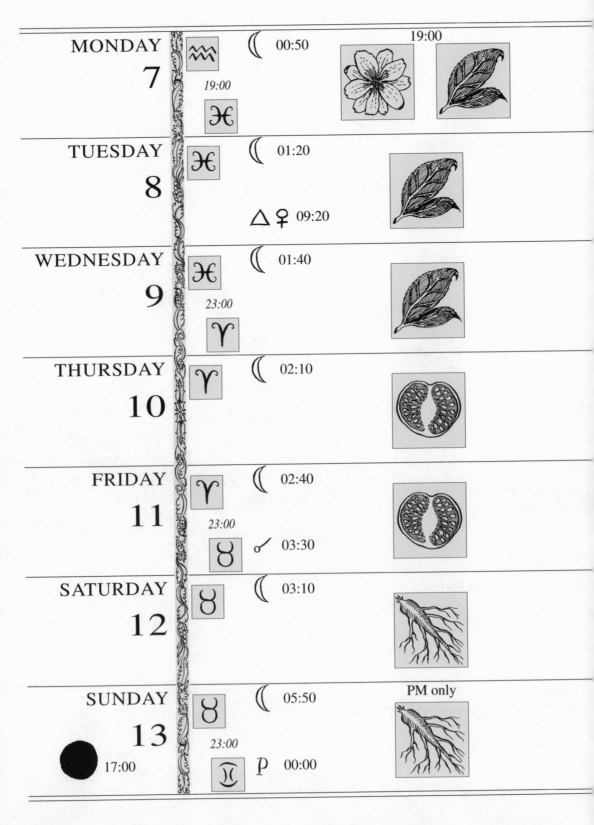

MONDAY 7	♒ *19:00* ♓	☽ 00:50	19:00
TUESDAY 8	♓	☽ 01:20 △ ♀ 09:20	
WEDNESDAY 9	♓ *23:00* ♈	☽ 01:40	
THURSDAY 10	♈	☽ 02:10	
FRIDAY 11	♈ *23:00* ♉	☽ 02:40 ♂ 03:30	
SATURDAY 12	♉	☽ 03:10	
SUNDAY 13	♉ *23:00* ♊	☽ 05:50 ♇ 00:00	PM only

17:00

JUNE

A change from flower to leaf elements early in the evening.

MONDAY

7

The Moon/Venus aspect is trine at the beginning of the working day.

TUESDAY

8

WEDNESDAY

9

THURSDAY

10

The Moon/Saturn aspect is conjunction (0°), a good day to work on perennials and trees.

FRIDAY

11

SATURDAY

12

The perigee of the Moon's orbit at the very outset of the day is the reason for suggesting planting in the afternoon only.

SUNDAY

13

 Libra
Air

 Scorpio
Water

 Sagittarius
Fire

 Capricorn
Earth

 Aquarius
Air

 Pisces
Water

JUNE

MONDAY **14**	♊	☽ 04:40	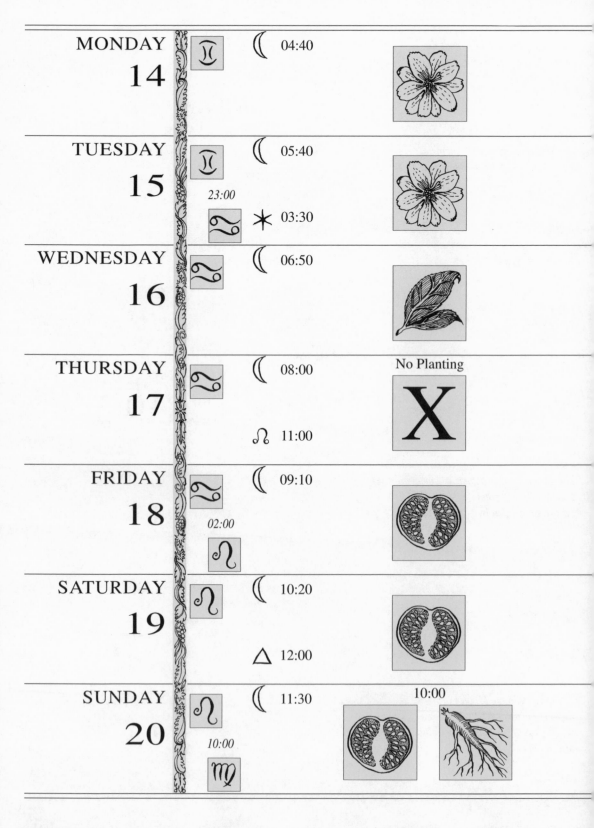
TUESDAY **15**	♊ *23:00* ♋	☽ 05:40 ✳ 03:30	
WEDNESDAY **16**	♋	☽ 06:50	
THURSDAY **17**	♋ ♌	☽ 08:00 11:00	No Planting **X**
FRIDAY **18**	♋ *02:00* ♌	☽ 09:10	
SATURDAY **19**	♌	☽ 10:20 △ 12:00	
SUNDAY **20**	♌ *10:00* ♍	☽ 11:30	10:00

♈ Aries *Fire*   ♉ Taurus *Earth*   ♊ Gemini *Air*   ♋ Cancer *Water*   ♌ Leo *Fire*   ♍ Virgo *Earth*

JUNE

MONDAY 14

The Moon/Saturn aspect is sextile (a good thing) early in the morning.

TUESDAY 15

Moonrise at the beginning of the working day: plan to synchronize as much as possible with this event.

WEDNESDAY 16

The Moon crossing its north node just before lunchtime is the reason for recommending no planting today.

THURSDAY 17

The change from leaf (Water) to fruit/seed (Fire) happens at night, leaving the whole day free for fruiting and seed-bearing plants.

FRIDAY 18

There is a trine aspect between the Moon and Saturn at midday. Concentrate sowing and planting between the hours of 10:00 and 12:00.

SATURDAY 19

Change from fruit/seed plants to root (Earth element) plants late in the morning.

SUNDAY 20

 Libra
Air

 Scorpio
Water

 Sagittarius
Fire

 Capricorn
Earth

 Aquarius
Air

 Pisces
Water

JUNE

MONDAY 21 — ♍ ☽ 13:50

TUESDAY 22 — ♍ ☽ 14:50 — 20:00 ♎

WEDNESDAY 23 — ♎ ☽ 15:50 — △ ☉ 10:20

THURSDAY 24 — ♎ ☽ 17:00 — ☍ 10:30 — □ ♀ 18:30

FRIDAY 25 — ♎ ☽ 18:00 — 09:00 ♏ — A 16:00 — 09:00

SATURDAY 26 — ♏ ☽ 19:00

SUNDAY 27 — ♏ ☽ 20:00 — 21:00 ♐

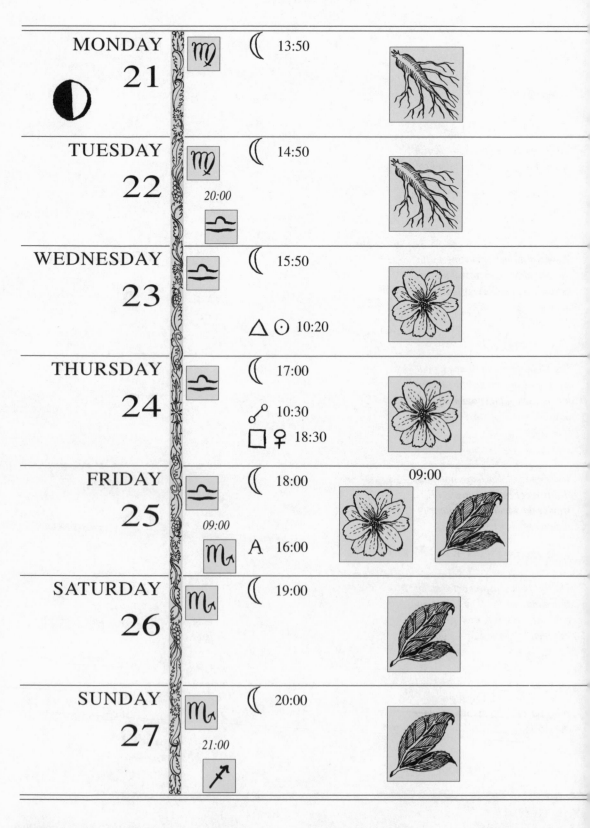

 Aries *Fire*   Taurus *Earth*   Gemini *Air*   Cancer *Water*   Leo *Fire*   Virgo *Earth*

JUNE

Midsummer, the longest day.	**MONDAY** **21**
	TUESDAY **22**
The Moon forms a trine aspect with the Sun. Remember that these solar aspects favour particularly the vineyard.	**WEDNESDAY** **23**
The Moon forms an oppositional aspect with Saturn and, later in the day, a square with Venus. This is an excellent flower day.	**THURSDAY** **24**
In the middle of the afternoon the Moon reaches the apogee of its orbit of the earth, a time of imbalance.	**FRIDAY** **25**
For best effect, work late in the afternoon.	**SATURDAY** **26**
	SUNDAY **27**

 Libra
Air

 Scorpio
Water

 Sagittarius
Fire

 Capricorn
Earth

 Aquarius
Air

 Pisces
Water

JUNE/JULY

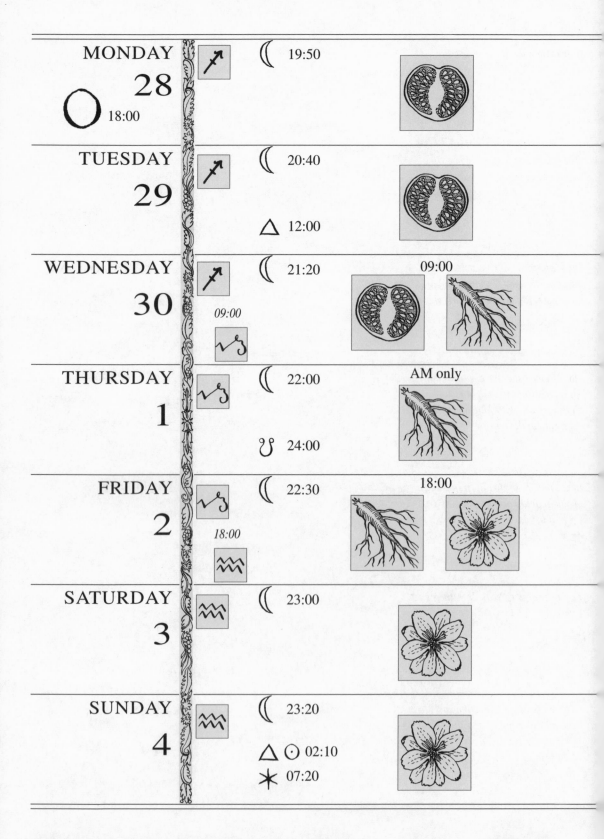

MONDAY 28 ♐ ○ 18:00 ☾ 19:50

TUESDAY 29 ♐ ☾ 20:40 △ 12:00

WEDNESDAY 30 ♐ ☾ 21:20 *09:00* ♑ — 09:00

THURSDAY 1 ♑ ☾ 22:00 ☋ 24:00 — AM only

FRIDAY 2 ♑ ☾ 22:30 *18:00* ♒ — 18:00

SATURDAY 3 ♒ ☾ 23:00

SUNDAY 4 ♒ ☾ 23:20 △ ☉ 02:10 ✳ 07:20

 Aries *Fire*   Taurus *Earth*   Gemini *Air*   Cancer *Water*   Leo *Fire*   Virgo *Earth*

JUNE/JULY

Full Moon at six o'clock in the evening.	**MONDAY** **28**
The Moon and Saturn form a trine aspect at midday. A good day for work, particularly in the afternoon.	**TUESDAY** **29**
The shift of elements is at the beginning of the day so that the rest can be devoted to root crops.	**WEDNESDAY** **30**
The Moon crosses its south node at midnight, hence the recommendation to work only during the morning.	**THURSDAY** **1**
The change in elements happens at the end of the working day.	**FRIDAY** **2**
	SATURDAY **3**
There is a Moon/Sun trine early in the morning hours and the Moon and Saturn are sextile (60°) a few hours later. A very good day for flowering plants and perennials.	**SUNDAY** **4**

 Libra *Air*   Scorpio *Water*   Sagittarius *Fire*   Capricorn *Earth*   Aquarius *Air*   Pisces *Water*

JULY

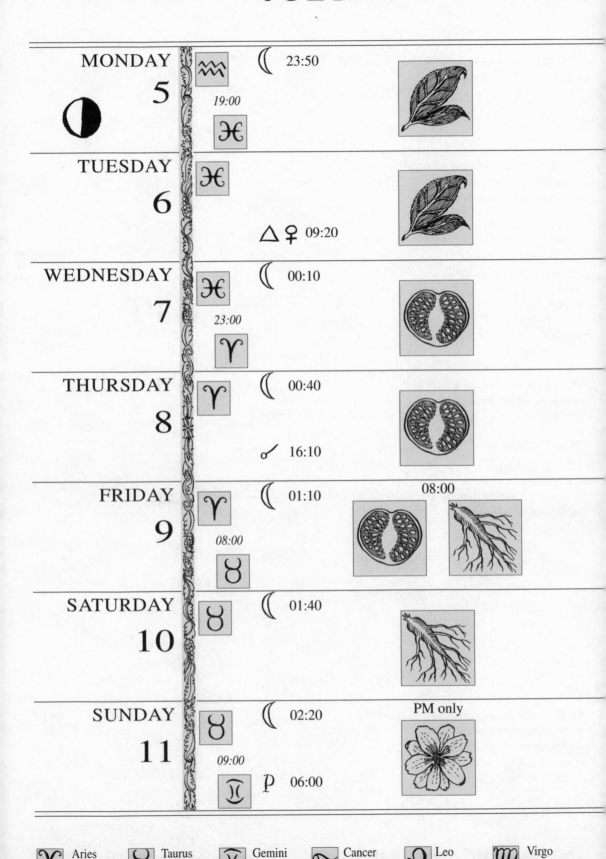

MONDAY **5**	♒	☽ 23:50	
	19:00 ♓		
TUESDAY **6**	♓	△ ♀ 09:20	
WEDNESDAY **7**	♓ *23:00* ♈	☽ 00:10	
THURSDAY **8**	♈	☽ 00:40 ♂ 16:10	
FRIDAY **9**	♈ *08:00* ♉	☽ 01:10	08:00
SATURDAY **10**	♉	☽ 01:40	
SUNDAY **11**	♉ *09:00* ♊	☽ 02:20 ♇ 06:00	PM only

♈ Aries *Fire*	♉ Taurus *Earth*	♊ Gemini *Air*	♋ Cancer *Water*	♌ Leo *Fire*	♍ Virgo *Earth*

JULY

A change from flower to leaf elements early in the morning, long before the day's work begins.	**MONDAY** **5**
This is an excellent flower day; make the most of it.	**TUESDAY** **6**
The change from Water to Fire element (leaf to fruit/seed) is at the beginning of the morning, leaving the whole day for the one type of plant.	**WEDNESDAY** **7**
The Moon/Saturn aspect is conjunction (0°) at the end of the afternoon.	**THURSDAY** **8**
The change from Fire to Earth element (fruit/seed to root) is at the beginning of the morning.	**FRIDAY** **9**
	SATURDAY **10**
The perigee of the Moon's orbit at the beginning of the day is the reason for suggesting planting in the afternoon only.	**SUNDAY** **11**

 Libra
Air

 Scorpio
Water

 Sagittarius
Fire

 Capricorn
Earth

 Aquarius
Air

 Pisces
Water

JULY

MONDAY **12**	♊ Gemini	☾ 03:20	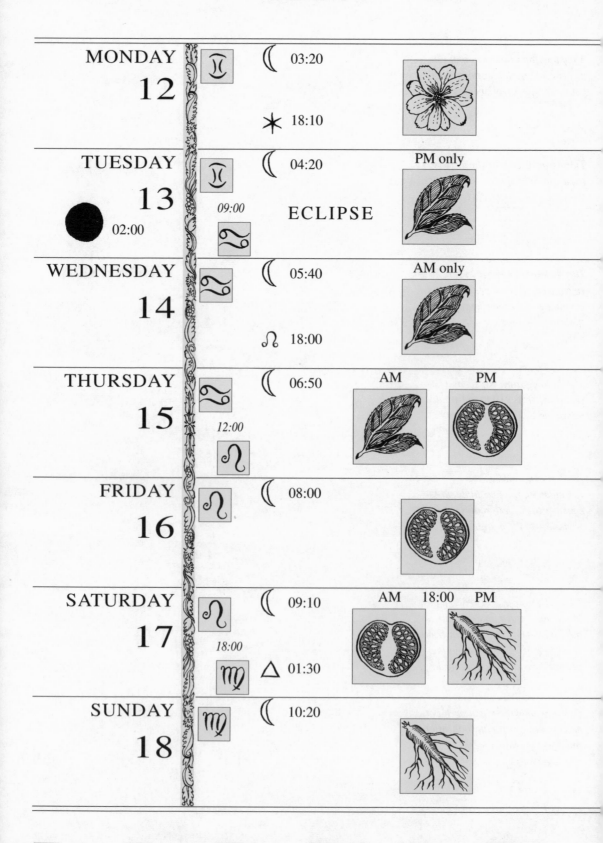
		✳ 18:10	
TUESDAY **13** ● 02:00	♊ Gemini *09:00* ♋ Cancer	☾ 04:20 **ECLIPSE**	PM only
WEDNESDAY **14**	♋ Cancer	☾ 05:40 ♌ 18:00	AM only
THURSDAY **15**	♋ Cancer *12:00* ♌ Leo	☾ 06:50	AM PM
FRIDAY **16**	♌ Leo	☾ 08:00	
SATURDAY **17**	♌ Leo *18:00* ♍ Virgo	☾ 09:10 △ 01:30	AM 18:00 PM
SUNDAY **18**	♍ Virgo	☾ 10:20	

 Aries *Fire*   Taurus *Earth*   Gemini *Air*   Cancer *Water*   Leo *Fire*   Virgo *Earth*

JULY

The Moon/Saturn aspect is sextile (a good thing) early in the evening.

MONDAY

12

There is an eclipse of the Moon in the early hours, hence no morning working.

TUESDAY

13

As the Moon passes through the north node at the beginning of evening, it is morning only for the plantsman.

WEDNESDAY

14

The change from leaf (Water) to fruit/seed (Fire) happens at mid-day, dividing the working day into equal parts.

THURSDAY

15

Moonrise at breakfast time; plant or sow in the first hours of the working day.

FRIDAY

16

There is a trine aspect between the Moon and Saturn in the middle of the night. The change from fruit (Fire) to root (Earth) elements happens at the end of the working day.

SATURDAY

17

Sow or work with root crops at the end of the morning, soon after moonrise.

SUNDAY

18

 Libra
Air

 Scorpio
Water

 Sagittarius
Fire

 Capricorn
Earth

 Aquarius
Air

 Pisces
Water

JULY

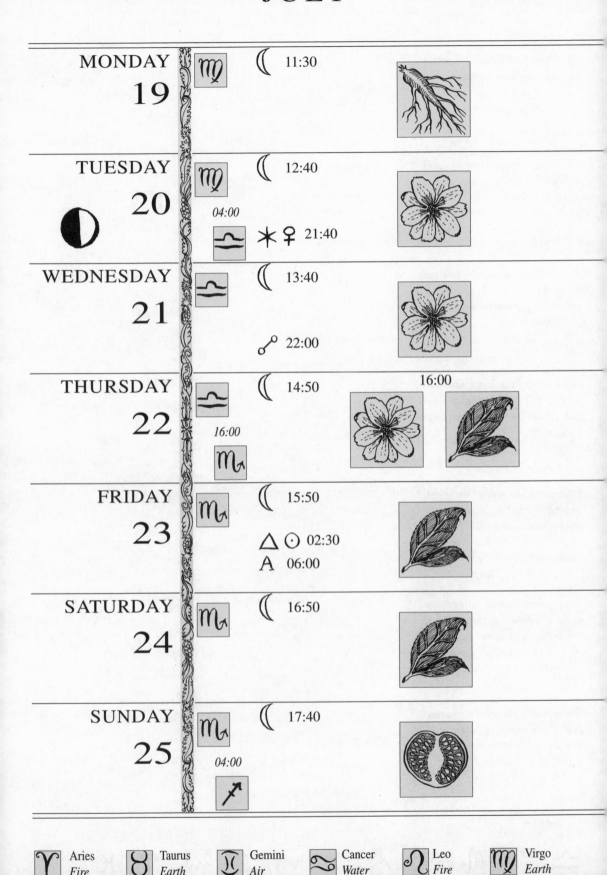

MONDAY **19**	♍	☽ 11:30	
TUESDAY **20** ◑	♍ *04:00* ♎	☽ 12:40 ✳ ♀ 21:40	
WEDNESDAY **21**	♎	☽ 13:40 ⚮ 22:00	
THURSDAY **22**	♎ *16:00* ♏	☽ 14:50 *16:00*	
FRIDAY **23**	♏	☽ 15:50 △ ☉ 02:30 A 06:00	
SATURDAY **24**	♏	☽ 16:50	
SUNDAY **25**	♏ *04:00* ♐	☽ 17:40	

♈ Aries *Fire*	♉ Taurus *Earth*	♊ Gemini *Air*	♋ Cancer *Water*	♌ Leo *Fire*	♍ Virgo *Earth*

JULY

Work especially at the end of the morning, as the Moon rises.	**MONDAY** **19**
The Moon and Venus are in sextile aspect. An especially good day for flowering plants.	**TUESDAY** **20**
The Moon forms an oppositional aspect with Saturn.	**WEDNESDAY** **21**
There is a change in elements half-way through the afternoon.	**THURSDAY** **22**
In the early morning, the Moon reaches the apogee of its orbit of the earth, a time of imbalance. The Moon forms a trine aspect with the Sun a few hours earlier.	**FRIDAY** **23**
Sor or plant leaf crops at the end of the afternoon, after moonrise.	**SATURDAY** **24**
The change in element occurs be-fore daybreak, thus leaving the whole day for working with fruit-ing and seeding plants.	**SUNDAY** **25**

 Libra
Air

 Scorpio
Water

 Sagittarius
Fire

 Capricorn
Earth

 Aquarius
Air

 Pisces
Water

JULY/AUGUST

MONDAY 26 ♐ ☽ 18:30

△ 22:50

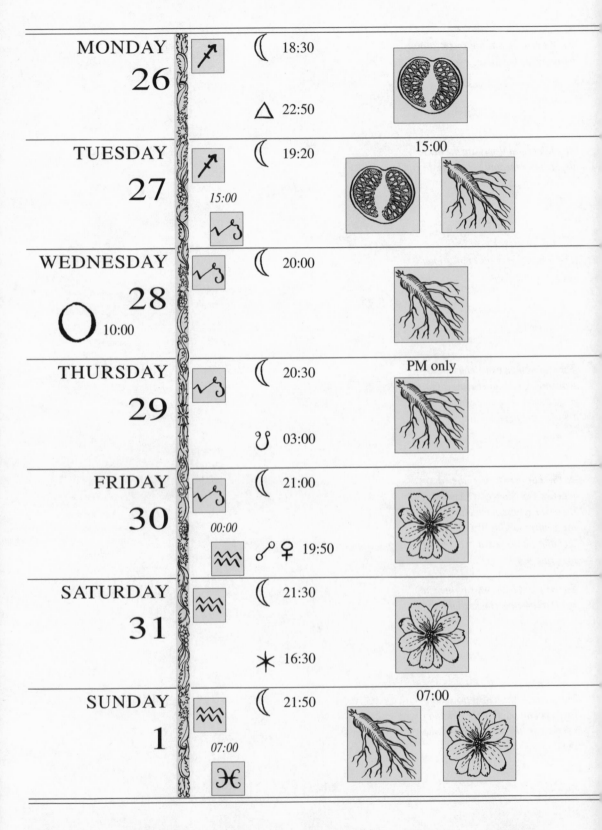

TUESDAY 27 ♐ ☽ 19:20

15:00

♏ 15:00

WEDNESDAY 28 ♏ ☽ 20:00

○ 10:00

THURSDAY 29 ♏ ☽ 20:30

PM only

☊ 03:00

FRIDAY 30 ♏ ☽ 21:00

00:00

♒ ☌ ♀ 19:50

SATURDAY 31 ♒ ☽ 21:30

✳ 16:30

SUNDAY 1 ♒ ☽ 21:50

07:00

07:00

♓

JULY/AUGUST

The Moon and Saturn form a trine aspect at the end of the evening.

MONDAY

26

The shift of elements is in the middle of the afternoon.

TUESDAY

27

WEDNESDAY

28

The Moon crosses its south node at three o'clock in the morning, hence the recommendation to work only during the afternoon.

THURSDAY

29

The change in elements happens at the outset of the day. The Moon forms an opposition with Venus during the evening. This is an especially good time to work with flowering plants.

FRIDAY

30

The Moon and Saturn form a sextile (60°) aspect towards the end of the afternoon.

SATURDAY

31

The progression from flowering plants to leaf plants (Air to Water) happens at the beginning of the working day.

SUNDAY

1

 Libra
Air

 Scorpio
Water

 Sagittarius
Fire

 Capricorn
Earth

 Aquarius
Air

 Pisces
Water

AUGUST

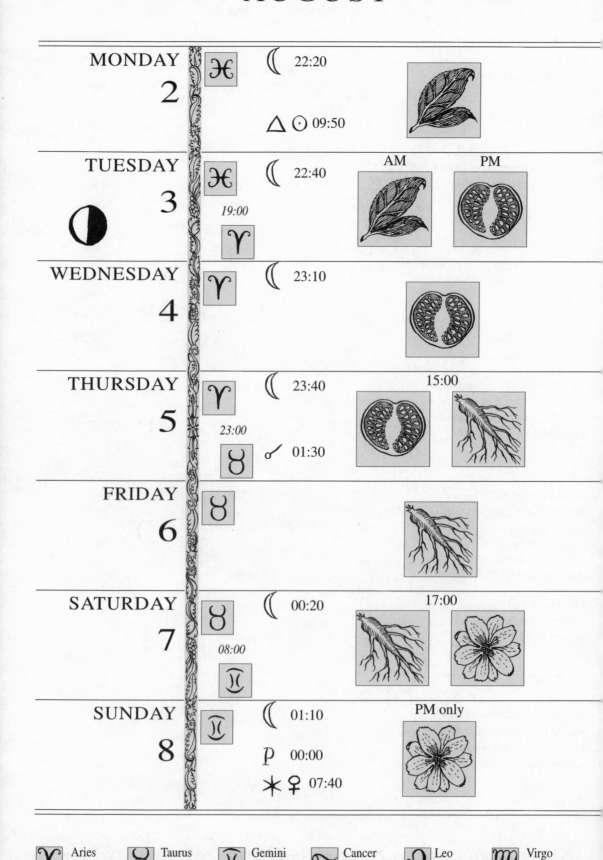

MONDAY **2**	♓	☾ 22:20 △ ☉ 09:50	
TUESDAY **3**	♓ *19:00* ♈	☾ 22:40	AM PM
WEDNESDAY **4**	♈	☾ 23:10	
THURSDAY **5**	♈ *23:00* ♉	☾ 23:40 ⚲ 01:30	15:00
FRIDAY **6**	♉		
SATURDAY **7**	♉ *08:00* ♊	☾ 00:20	17:00
SUNDAY **8**	♊	☾ 01:10 ♇ 00:00 ✶ ♀ 07:40	PM only

♈ Aries *Fire*	♉ Taurus *Earth*	♊ Gemini *Air*	♋ Cancer *Water*	♌ Leo *Fire*	♍ Virgo *Earth*

AUGUST

MONDAY

2

The Moon forms a trine aspect with the Sun in the morning.

TUESDAY

3

There is a change from Water to Fire element (leaf to fruit/seed).

WEDNESDAY

4

THURSDAY

5

The Moon/Saturn aspect is conjunction (0°). There is also a progression through the elements from fruit/seed to root plants.

FRIDAY

6

SATURDAY

7

There is a change from root to flowering plants at the end of the day's work.

SUNDAY

8

The perigee of the Moon's orbit at the beginning of the day is the reason for suggesting planting in the afternoon only. There is a Moon/Venus aspect of 60° (sextile) at about breakfast time.

 Libra
Air

 Scorpio
Water

 Sagittarius
Fire

 Capricorn
Earth

 Aquarius
Air

 Pisces
Water

AUGUST

MONDAY 9
Gemini ☿
☾ 02:10
19:00
Cancer ☾ ✳ 05:50
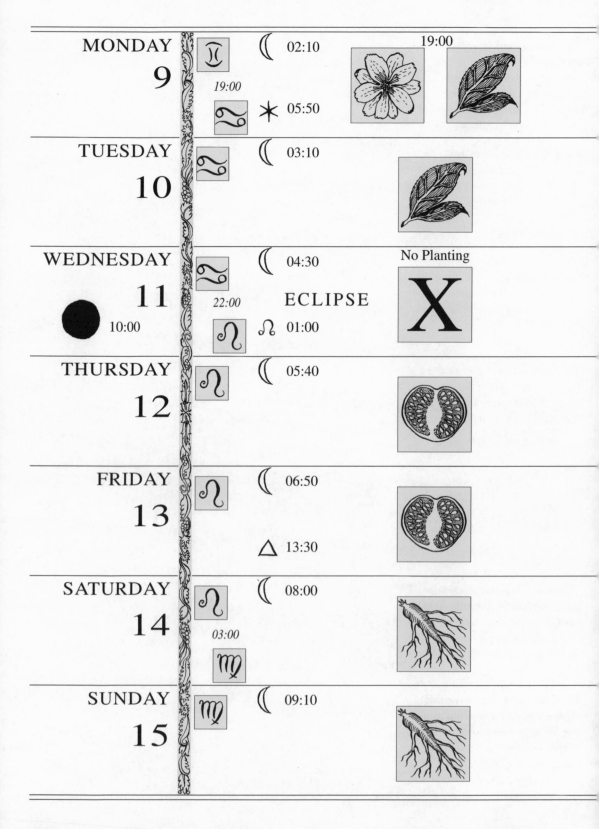
19:00

TUESDAY 10
Cancer ☾
☾ 03:10

WEDNESDAY 11
Cancer ☾
☾ 04:30
● 10:00
22:00
Leo ♌ ♌ 01:00
ECLIPSE
No Planting
X

THURSDAY 12
Leo ♌
☾ 05:40

FRIDAY 13
Leo ♌
☾ 06:50
△ 13:30

SATURDAY 14
Leo ♌
☾ 08:00
03:00
Virgo ♍

SUNDAY 15
Virgo ♍
☾ 09:10

 Aries
Fire   Taurus *Earth*   Gemini *Air*   Cancer *Water*   Leo *Fire*   Virgo *Earth*

AUGUST

MONDAY 9

The Moon/Saturn aspect is sextile (a good thing) early in the morning. At the other end of the day the elements change from those favouring flowering plants to those promoting leaf plants.

TUESDAY 10

WEDNESDAY 11

The Moon passes through the north node just after midnight; there is a solar eclipse in the middle of the morning. No planting is the order of the day.

THURSDAY 12

FRIDAY 13

There is a trine aspect between the Moon and Saturn at lunchtime. This is a particularly good day for working with fruit or seed plants.

SATURDAY 14

The change from fruit (Fire) to root (Earth) elements happens in the middle of the night, leaving the whole day for root plants.

SUNDAY 15

With moonrise during working hours, try to concentrate any plans on one hour either side of that event.

 Libra
Air

 Scorpio
Water

 Sagittarius
Fire

 Capricorn
Earth

 Aquarius
Air

 Pisces
Water

AUGUST

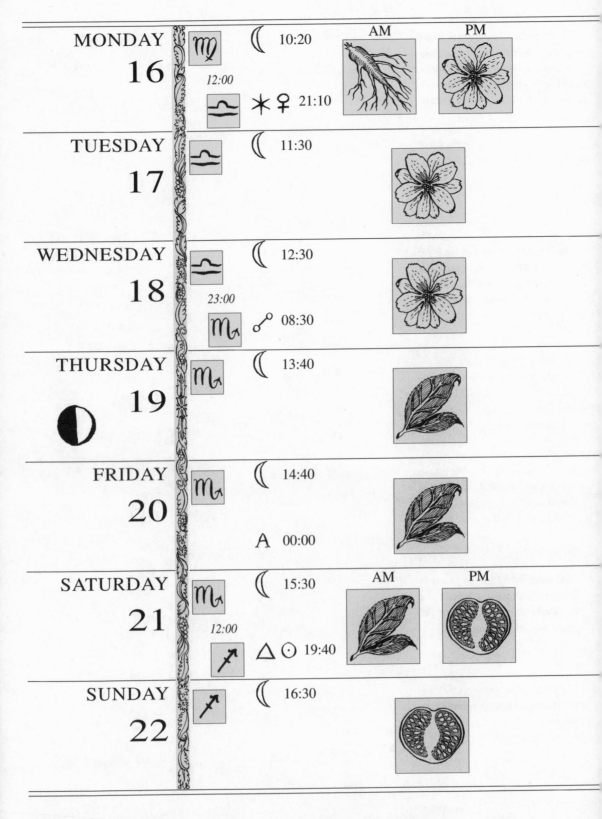

MONDAY 16 ♍ ☽ 10:20 — AM / PM
12:00 ♎ ✳ ♀ 21:10

TUESDAY 17 ♎ ☽ 11:30

WEDNESDAY 18 ♎ ☽ 12:30
23:00 ♏ ☌ 08:30

THURSDAY 19 ♏ ☽ 13:40

FRIDAY 20 ♏ ☽ 14:40
A 00:00

SATURDAY 21 ♏ ☽ 15:30 — AM / PM
12:00 ♐ △ ☉ 19:40

SUNDAY 22 ♐ ☽ 16:30

 Aries *Fire*   **Taurus** *Earth*   **Gemini** *Air*   **Cancer** *Water*   **Leo** *Fire*   **Virgo** *Earth*

AUGUST

The Moon and Venus are in sextile aspect. The shift from one element to another happens in the middle of the day.

MONDAY
16

The midday period is the best time to work with flowering plants.

TUESDAY
17

The Moon forms an oppositional aspect with Saturn. There is a change in elements in the very late evening, leaving the whole day to deal with flowering plants.

WEDNESDAY
18

The hours between lunch and tea are the best for work (moonrise being the hour it is). Think, perhaps, of successional sowings of saladings and herbs.

THURSDAY
19

In the early morning, the Moon reaches the apogee of its orbit of the earth, a time of imbalance.

FRIDAY
20

There is a shift from leaf plants to fruit/seed plants at midday. The Moon forms a trine aspect with the Sun during the evening hours.

SATURDAY
21

The afternoon moonrise is the time to concentrate on any sowing or planting.

SUNDAY
22

 Libra
Air

 Scorpio
Water

 Sagittarius
Fire

 Capricorn
Earth

 Aquarius
Air

 Pisces
Water

AUGUST

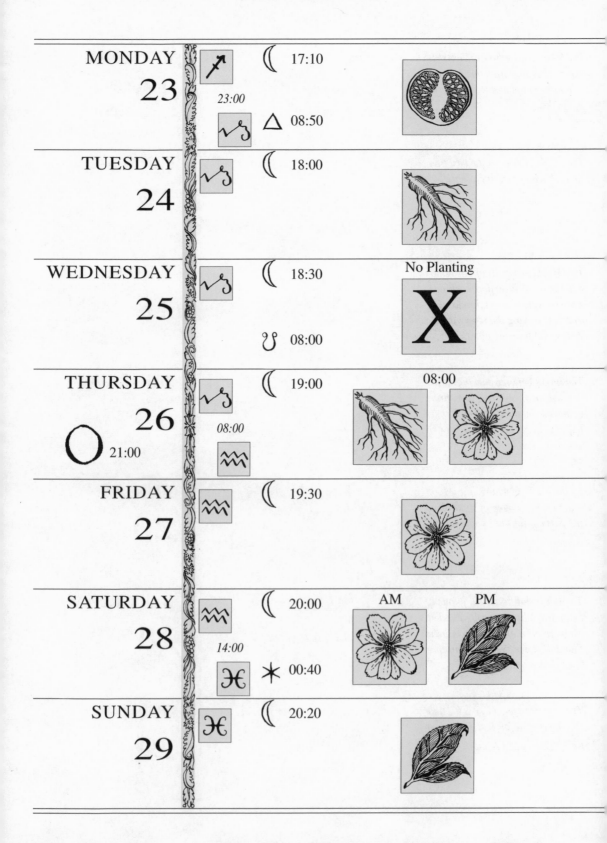

MONDAY 23 — ♐ ☾ 17:10 — *23:00* ♑ △ 08:50

TUESDAY 24 — ♑ ☾ 18:00

WEDNESDAY 25 — ♑ ☾ 18:30 — ♎ 08:00 — No Planting **X**

THURSDAY 26 — ♑ ☾ 19:00 — ○ 21:00 — *08:00* ♒ — 08:00

FRIDAY 27 — ♒ ☾ 19:30

SATURDAY 28 — ♒ ☾ 20:00 — *14:00* ♓ ✳ 00:40 — AM / PM

SUNDAY 29 — ♓ ☾ 20:20

♈ Aries *Fire*   ♉ Taurus *Earth*   ♊ Gemini *Air*   ♋ Cancer *Water*   ♌ Leo *Fire*   ♍ Virgo *Earth*

AUGUST

The Moon and Saturn form a trine aspect. The shift of elements is in the middle of the night.

MONDAY

23

TUESDAY

24

The Moon crosses its south node at eight o'clock in the morning, hence the recommendation to suspend sowing and planting for the day.

WEDNESDAY

25

The change in elements happens at the outset of the working day. Full Moon early in the night.

THURSDAY

26

FRIDAY

27

The Moon and Saturn form a sextile (60°) aspect in the middle of the night. The ruling signs change at lunchtime dividing the day into two halves.

SATURDAY

28

SUNDAY

29

 Libra
Air

 Scorpio
Water

 Sagittarius
Fire

 Capricorn
Earth

 Aquarius
Air

 Pisces
Water

AUGUST/SEPTEMBER

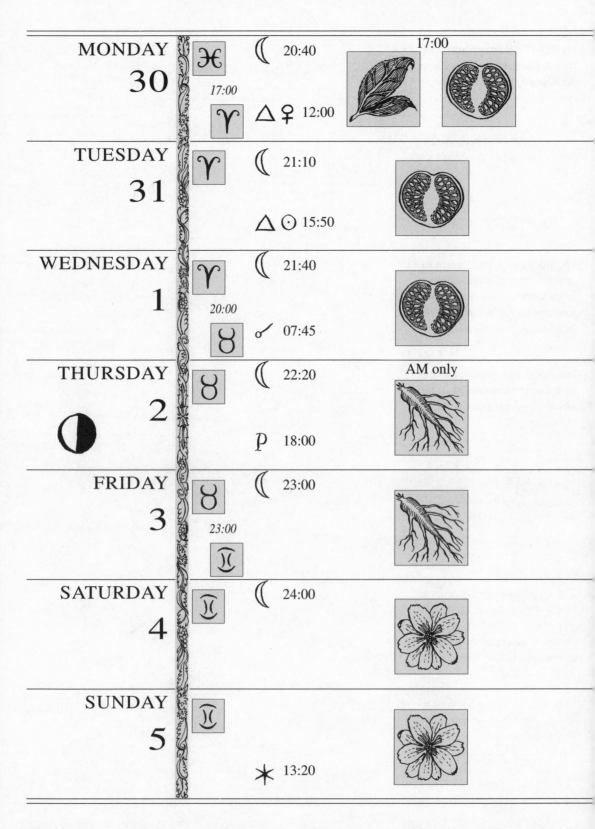

MONDAY 30 ♓ ☾ 20:40 — 17:00

17:00 ♈ △ ♀ 12:00

TUESDAY 31 ♈ ☾ 21:10 — △ ☉ 15:50

WEDNESDAY 1 ♈ ☾ 21:40 — *20:00* ♉ ☌ 07:45

THURSDAY 2 ♉ ☾ 22:20 — AM only — ♇ 18:00

FRIDAY 3 ♉ ☾ 23:00 — *23:00* ♊

SATURDAY 4 ♊ ☾ 24:00

SUNDAY 5 ♊ ✳ 13:20

AUGUST/SEPTEMBER

MONDAY 30

The Moon forms a trine aspect with Venus at midday. There is a change from Water to Fire element (leaf to fruit/seed).

TUESDAY 31

The Moon forms a trine aspect with the Sun in the afternoon.

WEDNESDAY 1

The Moon/Saturn aspect is conjunction (0°). There is also a progression through the elements from fruit/seed to root plants after the end of the working day.

THURSDAY 2

The perigee of the Moon's orbit at the beginning of the evening is the reason for suggesting planting in the morning only.

FRIDAY 3

There is a change from root to flowering plants at the end of the day's work.

SATURDAY 4

SUNDAY 5

There is a Moon/Saturn aspect of 60° (sextile) at about lunchtime. This is a good day to work with perennials.

 Libra
Air

 Scorpio
Water

 Sagittarius
Fire

 Capricorn
Earth

 Aquarius
Air

Pisces
Water

SEPTEMBER

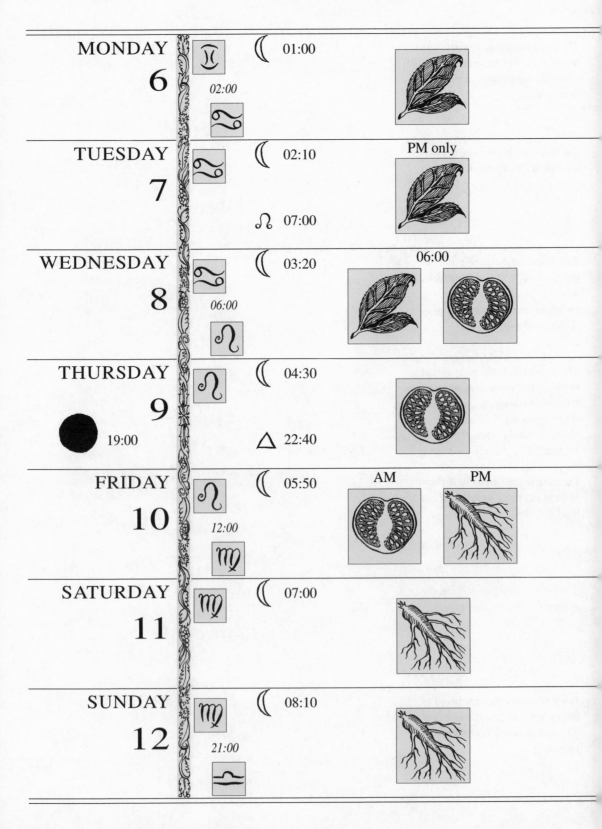

MONDAY 6 — Gemini ☾ 01:00 — 02:00 Cancer

TUESDAY 7 — Cancer ☾ 02:10 — ♌ 07:00 — PM only

WEDNESDAY 8 — Cancer ☾ 03:20 — 06:00 Leo — 06:00

THURSDAY 9 — Leo ☾ 04:30 — ● 19:00 — △ 22:40

FRIDAY 10 — Leo ☾ 05:50 — 12:00 Virgo — AM / PM

SATURDAY 11 — Virgo ☾ 07:00

SUNDAY 12 — Virgo ☾ 08:10 — 21:00 Libra

SEPTEMBER

The elements change from those favouring flowering plants to those promoting leaf plants in the middle of the night.

MONDAY
6

The Moon passes through the north node early in the morning: no planting until the afternoon.

TUESDAY
7

The progression through the ruling signs, from leaf plants to fruit or seed plants, occurs at the beginning of the working day.

WEDNESDAY
8

New Moon. There is a trine aspect between the Moon and Saturn in the early hours of the night. This is the day (9.9.99) the millennium bug starts to race. Stay off the tractor today.

THURSDAY
9

The change from fruit (Fire) to root (Earth) elements happens in the middle of the day.

FRIDAY
10

A good day to harvest crops for storage – when the Moon is new.

SATURDAY
11

The change in elements happens during the evening, so the whole day may be devoted to your root crops.

SUNDAY
12

 Libra
Air

 Scorpio
Water

 Sagittarius
Fire

 Capricorn
Earth

 Aquarius
Air

 Pisces
Water

SEPTEMBER

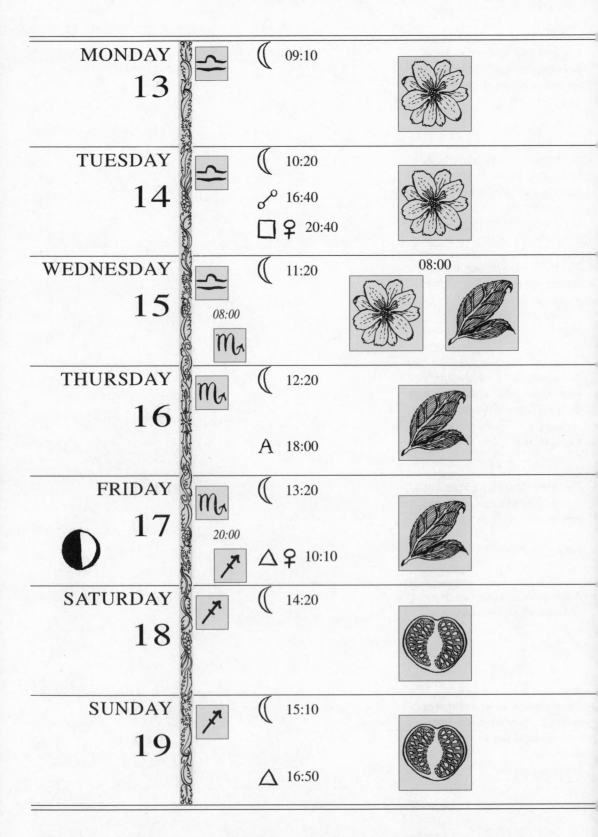

MONDAY 13 — ♎ — ☽ 09:10

TUESDAY 14 — ♎ — ☽ 10:20 — ☍ 16:40 — □ ♀ 20:40

WEDNESDAY 15 — ♎ — ☽ 11:20 — 08:00 ♏ — 08:00

THURSDAY 16 — ♏ — ☽ 12:20 — A 18:00

FRIDAY 17 — ♏ — ☽ 13:20 — 20:00 ♐ — △ ♀ 10:10

SATURDAY 18 — ♐ — ☽ 14:20

SUNDAY 19 — ♐ — ☽ 15:10 — △ 16:50

SEPTEMBER

Any work with flowering plants is best done in the hours before lunch (to take advantage of moonrise).

MONDAY
13

The Moon forms an oppositional aspect with Saturn. The Moon and Venus are square. This is a very good flower day, either between 10:00 and 12:00, or very late in the afternoon.

TUESDAY
14

There is a change in elements in the morning.

WEDNESDAY
15

In the early evening, the Moon reaches the apogee of its orbit of the earth, a time of imbalance.

THURSDAY
16

There is a shift of element from leaf to fruit/seed plants after the working day. The Moon forms a trine aspect with Venus during the evening.

FRIDAY
17

The best time to work is between 13:00 and 15:00.

SATURDAY
18

The Moon and Saturn are trine in the middle of the afternoon. An especially good day to work with trees and perennials; 15:00 to 17:00 the best time.

SUNDAY
19

 Libra
Air

 Scorpio
Water

 Sagittarius
Fire

 Capricorn
Earth

 Aquarius
Air

 Pisces
Water

SEPTEMBER

MONDAY 20

♐ 08:00

♑

☾ 15:50

△ ☉ 13:00

08:00

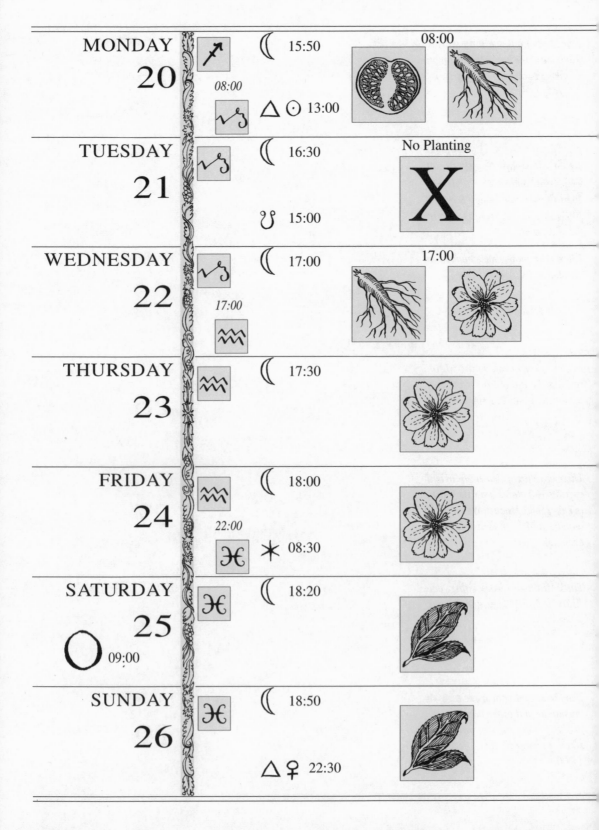

TUESDAY 21

♑

☾ 16:30

☋ 15:00

No Planting

X

WEDNESDAY 22

♑ 17:00

♒

☾ 17:00

17:00

THURSDAY 23

♒

☾ 17:30

FRIDAY 24

♒ 22:00

♓

☾ 18:00

⚹ 08:30

SATURDAY 25

♓

☾ 18:20

○ 09:00

SUNDAY 26

♓

☾ 18:50

△ ♀ 22:30

SEPTEMBER

The Moon and Sun form a trine. The shift of elements is at the beginning of the working day.

MONDAY

20

The Moon crosses its south node in the middle of the afternoon, hence the recommendation to suspend sowing and planting for the day.

TUESDAY

21

The change in elements happens at the end of the working day.

WEDNESDAY

22

THURSDAY

23

The Moon and Saturn form a sextile (60°) aspect. The ruling signs change late in the evening. A good day to work with perennials.

FRIDAY

24

Full Moon in the morning. The Harvest Moon: gather leaf crops.

SATURDAY

25

The Moon forms a trine with Venus at the end of the evening.

SUNDAY

26

 Libra
Air

 Scorpio
Water

 Sagittarius
Fire

 Capricorn
Earth

 Aquarius
Air

 Pisces
Water

SEPTEMBER/OCTOBER

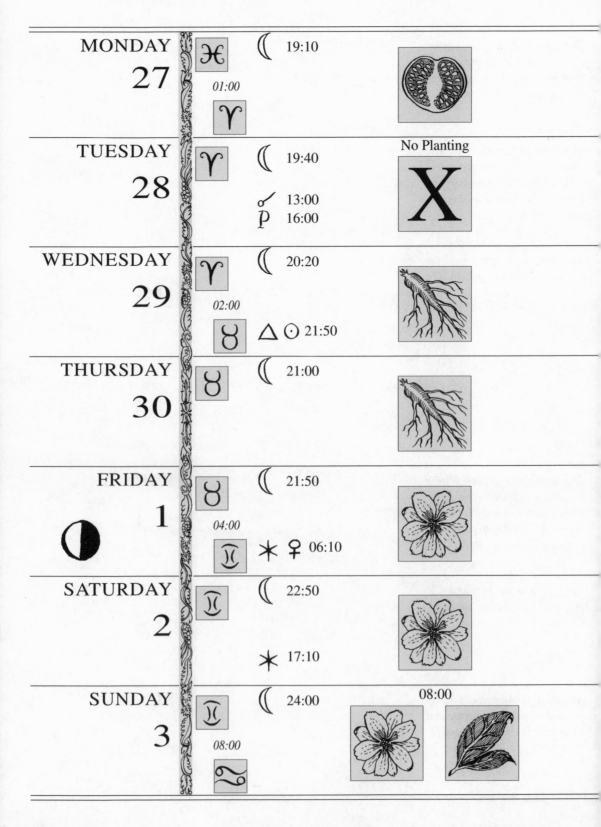

MONDAY 27   ♓   ☾ 19:10

01:00

♈

TUESDAY 28   ♈   ☾ 19:40

☌ 13:00
P 16:00

No Planting

X

WEDNESDAY 29   ♈   ☾ 20:20

02:00

♉   △ ☉ 21:50

THURSDAY 30   ♉   ☾ 21:00

FRIDAY 1   ♉   ☾ 21:50

04:00

♊   ✳ ♀ 06:10

SATURDAY 2   ♊   ☾ 22:50

✳ 17:10

SUNDAY 3   ♊   ☾ 24:00

08:00

08:00

♋

Aries *Fire*	Taurus *Earth*	Gemini *Air*	Cancer *Water*	Leo *Fire*	Virgo *Earth*

SEPTEMBER/OCTOBER

There is a change from water to fire element (leaf to fruit/seed) during the night hours. This is a good time to harvest fruit to eat or to sell.

MONDAY

27

The Moon forms a conjunction with Saturn in the afternoon, closely followed by it reaching the perigee of its orbit of the earth, a time of imbalance, hence no planting today.

TUESDAY

28

There is a progression through the elements from fruit/seed to root plants during the night; the Moon forms a trine aspect with the Sun well after working hours.

WEDNESDAY

29

THURSDAY

30

There is a change of element from root to flowering plants. The Moon forms a sextile aspect with Venus. This is a good day to work with flowering plants.

FRIDAY

1

There is a Moon/Saturn aspect of 60° (sextile) at the end of the afternoon.

SATURDAY

2

Just before breakfast, the ruling element changes from Air (fruit and seed plants) to Water (leaf and foliage plants).

SUNDAY

3

 Libra *Air*

 Scorpio *Water*

 Sagittarius *Fire*

 Capricorn *Earth*

 Aquarius *Air*

 Pisces *Water*

OCTOBER

MONDAY 4
♋   ♌ 11:00   No Planting   X

TUESDAY 5
♋   ☽ 01:10   06:00
06:00
♌
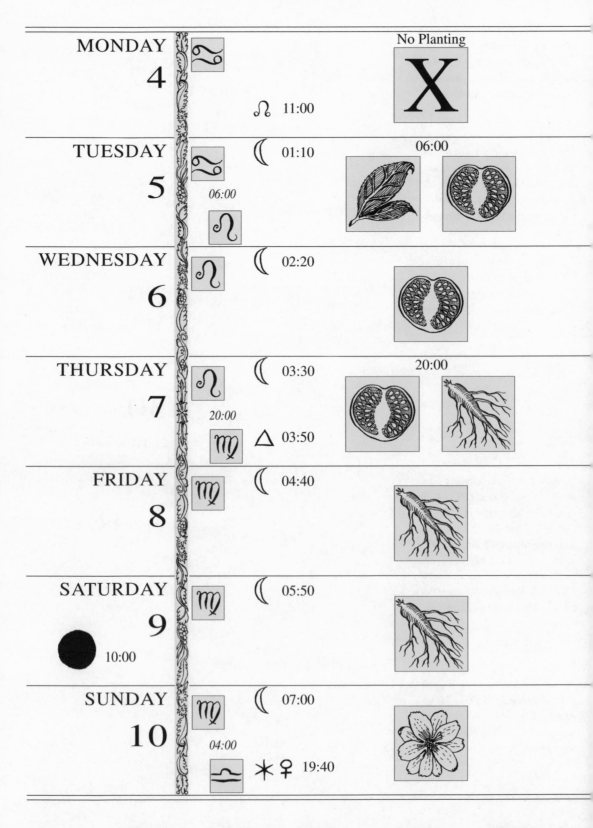

WEDNESDAY 6
♌   ☽ 02:20

THURSDAY 7
♌   ☽ 03:30   20:00
20:00
♍   △ 03:50

FRIDAY 8
♍   ☽ 04:40

SATURDAY 9
♍   ☽ 05:50
● 10:00

SUNDAY 10
♍   ☽ 07:00
04:00
♎   ✳ ♀ 19:40

 Aries *Fire*   Taurus *Earth*   Gemini *Air*   Cancer *Water*   Leo *Fire*   Virgo *Earth*

OCTOBER

The Moon passes through the north node in the morning: no planting.

MONDAY

4

The progression through the ruling signs, from leaf plants to fruit or seed plants, occurs in the middle of the working day.

TUESDAY

5

WEDNESDAY

6

There is a trine aspect between the Moon and Saturn in the early hours of the morning. The change from fruit (Fire) to root (Earth) element happens in the middle of the evening.

THURSDAY

7

Both today and tomorrow are good days to harvest root crops for storage (when the Moon is new).

FRIDAY

8

SATURDAY

9

The change in element happens during the night so the whole day may be devoted to flowering crops. There is a sextile aspect between the Moon and Venus at the beginning of the evening.

SUNDAY

10

 Libra
Air

 Scorpio
Water

 Sagittarius
Fire

 Capricorn
Earth

 Aquarius
Air

 Pisces
Water

OCTOBER

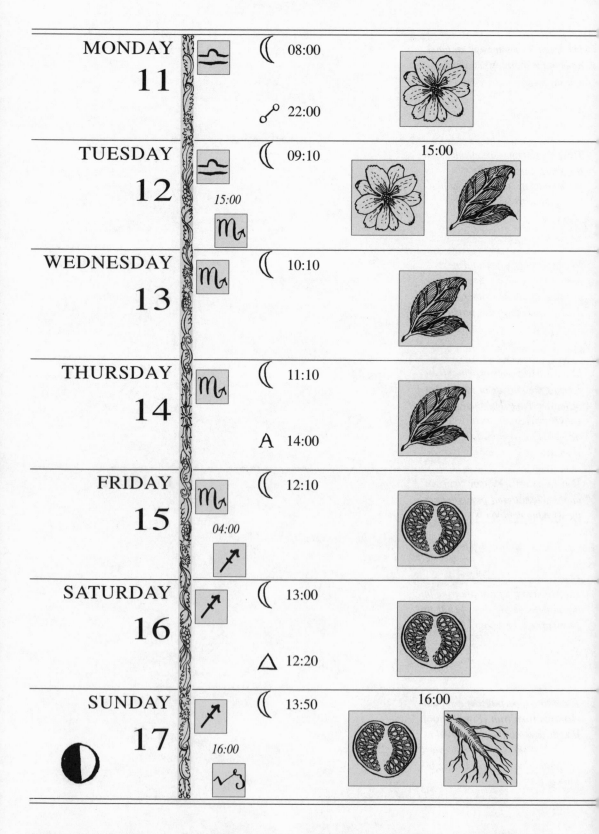

MONDAY 11

🌙 08:00

☌ 22:00

TUESDAY 12

🌙 09:10

15:00

15:00

♏

WEDNESDAY 13

♏ 🌙 10:10

THURSDAY 14

♏ 🌙 11:10

A 14:00

FRIDAY 15

♏ 🌙 12:10

04:00

♐

SATURDAY 16

♐ 🌙 13:00

△ 12:20

SUNDAY 17

♐ 🌙 13:50

16:00

16:00

♑

OCTOBER

The Moon forms an oppositional aspect with Saturn. Work with trees and shrubs.	**MONDAY** **11**
There is a change in elements in the afternoon.	**TUESDAY** **12**
Moonrise this week and next is during the working day. Remember that the hours either side of moonrise are the most productive for any sowing or planting.	**WEDNESDAY** **13**
In the early afternoon, the Moon reaches the apogee of its orbit of the earth, a time of imbalance.	**THURSDAY** **14**
There is a shift of element from leaf plants to fruit/seed plants before the working day.	**FRIDAY** **15**
The Moon and Saturn are trine in the middle of the day. 12:00 to 14:00 are the best hours for work.	**SATURDAY** **16**
The ruling signs indicate a shift in elements from fruit (Fire) to root (Earth) towards the end of the day.	**SUNDAY** **17**

 Libra
Air

 Scorpio
Water

 Sagittarius
Fire

 Capricorn
Earth

 Aquarius
Air

 Pisces
Water

OCTOBER

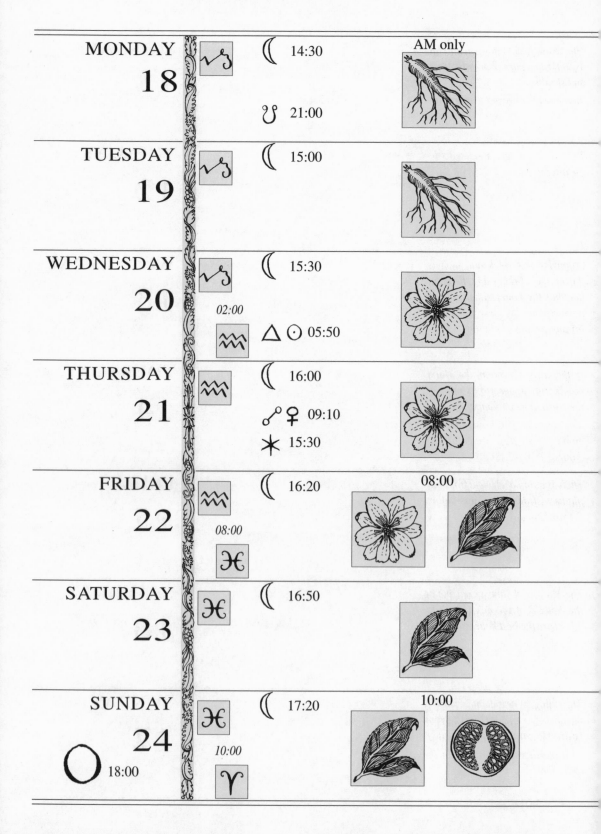

MONDAY **18**	♑	☾ 14:30 ☋ 21:00	AM only
TUESDAY **19**	♑	☾ 15:00	
WEDNESDAY **20**	♑ *02:00* ♒	☾ 15:30 △ ☉ 05:50	
THURSDAY **21**	♒	☾ 16:00 ☍ ♀ 09:10 ✳ 15:30	
FRIDAY **22**	♒ *08:00* ♓	☾ 16:20	08:00
SATURDAY **23**	♓	☾ 16:50	
SUNDAY **24** ○ 18:00	♓ *10:00* ♈	☾ 17:20	10:00

 Aries *Fire*   Taurus *Earth*   Gemini *Air*   Cancer *Water*   Leo *Fire*   Virgo *Earth*

OCTOBER

The Moon crosses the dragon's tail (south node) in the middle of the evening, hence the recommendation to work only in the morning.

MONDAY

18

TUESDAY

19

The change in elements happens in the middle of the night. The Moon and Sun form a trine aspect.

WEDNESDAY

20

The Moon and Saturn form a sextile (60°) aspect. The Moon is in opposition (180°) to Venus a few hours earlier. This is an especially good flower day, above all the hours 15:00–17:00.

THURSDAY

21

The ruling signs change quite early in the morning.

FRIDAY

22

The approach of Full Moon is a fine time to think of harvesting.

SATURDAY

23

Full Moon in the evening. There is progression from leaf (Water) to fruit- and seed-bearing plants (Fire). Harvest especially in the afternoon.

SUNDAY

24

 Libra
Air

 Scorpio
Water

 Sagittarius
Fire

 Capricorn
Earth

 Aquarius
Air

 Pisces
Water

OCTOBER

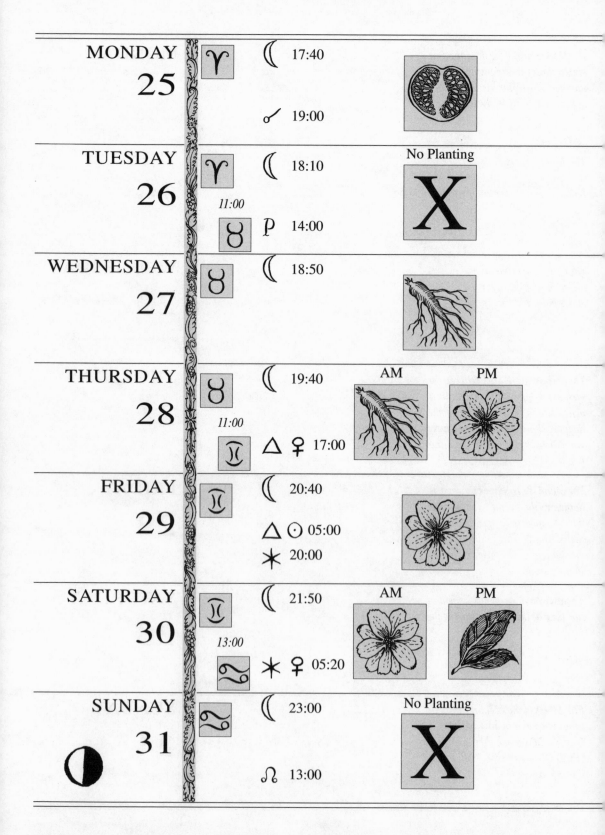

MONDAY 25
♈ ☾ 17:40
♂ 19:00

TUESDAY 26
♈ ☾ 18:10
11:00
♉ ♇ 14:00
No Planting
X

WEDNESDAY 27
♉ ☾ 18:50

THURSDAY 28
♉ ☾ 19:40
11:00
♊ △ ♀ 17:00
AM   PM

FRIDAY 29
♊ ☾ 20:40
△ ☉ 05:00
✳ 20:00

SATURDAY 30
♊ ☾ 21:50
13:00
♋ ✳ ♀ 05:20
AM   PM

SUNDAY 31
♋ ☾ 23:00
♌ 13:00
No Planting
X

 Aries *Fire*   Taurus *Earth*   Gemini *Air*   Cancer *Water*   Leo *Fire*   Virgo *Earth*

OCTOBER

The Moon forms a conjunction with Saturn in the evening. This is another good day for harvesting seeds for the following season.

MONDAY

25

The Moon reaches the perigee of its orbit of the earth, a time of imbalance, hence no planting today.

TUESDAY

26

WEDNESDAY

27

There is a progression through the elements from root plants to flowering plants in the middle of the day; the Moon forms a trine aspect with Venus at the end of the afternoon.

THURSDAY

28

The Moon is in a sextile aspect with Saturn in the evening and formed a trine aspect with the Sun early in the morning. This is an excellent combination of events for working in the garden.

FRIDAY

29

There is a Moon/Venus aspect of 60° (sextile) before the start of the working day.

SATURDAY

30

The Moon crosses its north node at midday so no planting today.

SUNDAY

31

 Libra
Air

 Scorpio
Water

 Sagittarius
Fire

 Capricorn
Earth

 Aquarius
Air

 Pisces
Water

NOVEMBER

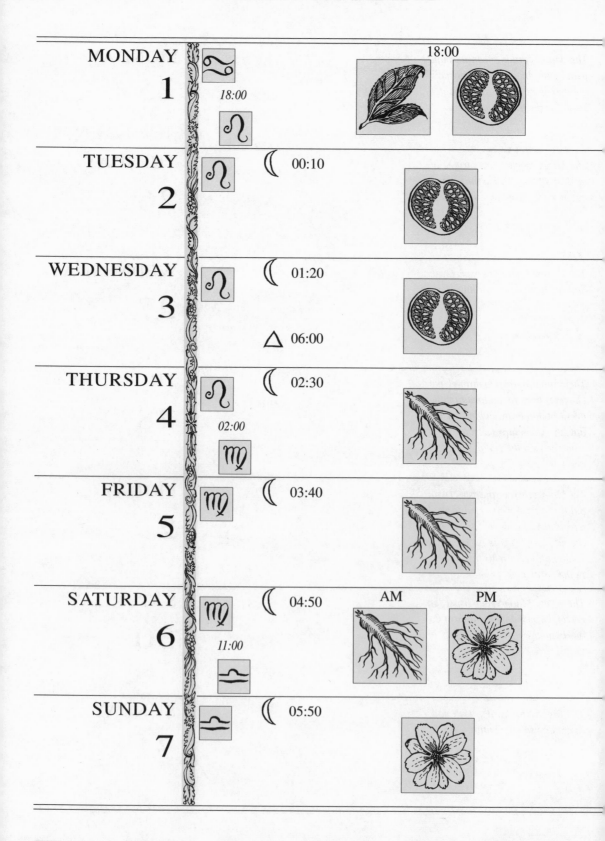

MONDAY 1

♌   *18:00*   ♌

       18:00

TUESDAY 2

♌   ☾ 00:10

WEDNESDAY 3

♌   ☾ 01:20

    △ 06:00

THURSDAY 4

♌   ☾ 02:30

   02:00   ♍

FRIDAY 5

♍   ☾ 03:40

SATURDAY 6

♍   ☾ 04:50   AM   PM

   11:00   ♎

SUNDAY 7

♎   ☾ 05:50

NOVEMBER

The change in ruling elements happens at the end of the working day.

MONDAY

1

TUESDAY

2

The Moon forms a trine aspect with Saturn early in the morning.

WEDNESDAY

3

The change from fruit (Fire) to root (Earth) element happens in the middle of the night, leaving the day for the one plant type.

THURSDAY

4

FRIDAY

5

The change in elements is at the end of the morning, so the day may be divided between two sorts of crops.

SATURDAY

6

SUNDAY

7

 Libra
Air

 Scorpio
Water

 Sagittarius
Fire

 Capricorn
Earth

 Aquarius
Air

 Pisces
Water

NOVEMBER

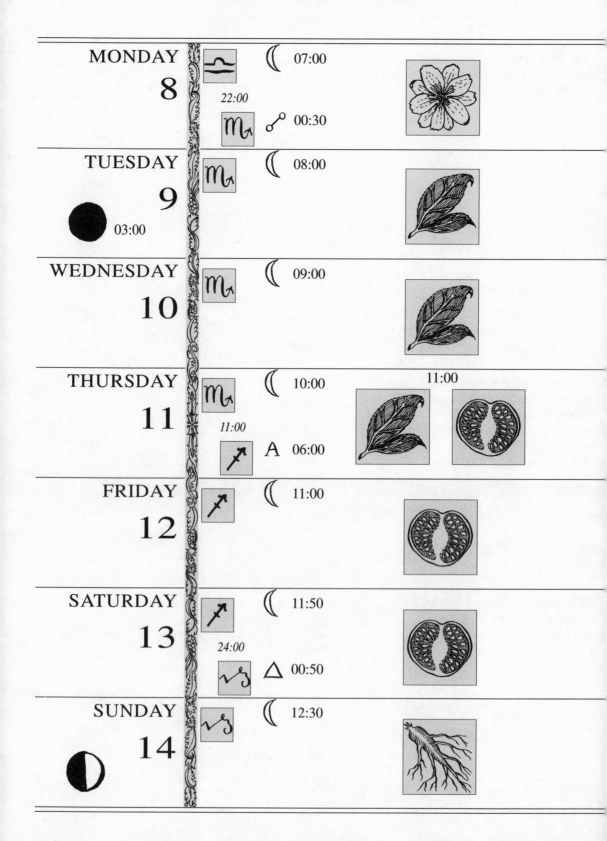

MONDAY 8	♎ 22:00 ♏	☾ 07:00 ☌ 00:30	
TUESDAY 9 ● 03:00	♏	☾ 08:00	
WEDNESDAY 10	♏	☾ 09:00	
THURSDAY 11	♏ 11:00 ♐	☾ 10:00 A 06:00	11:00
FRIDAY 12	♐	☾ 11:00	
SATURDAY 13	♐ 24:00 ♑	☾ 11:50 △ 00:50	
SUNDAY 14 ◑	♑	☾ 12:30	

NOVEMBER

The Moon forms an oppositional aspect with Saturn. There is a change in elements in the evening.

MONDAY

8

Take advantage of the fact that moonrise is during working hours during the coming days.

TUESDAY

9

WEDNESDAY

10

In the late afternoon, the Moon reaches the apogee of its orbit of the earth, a time of imbalance. There is a shift of element from leaf plants to fruit/seed plants in the middle of the day.

THURSDAY

11

The hours 10:00–12:00 are the best for working.

FRIDAY

12

The Moon and Saturn are trine in the middle of the night.

SATURDAY

13

SUNDAY

14

 Libra
Air

 Scorpio
Water

 Sagittarius
Fire

 Capricorn
Earth

 Aquarius
Air

 Pisces
Water

NOVEMBER

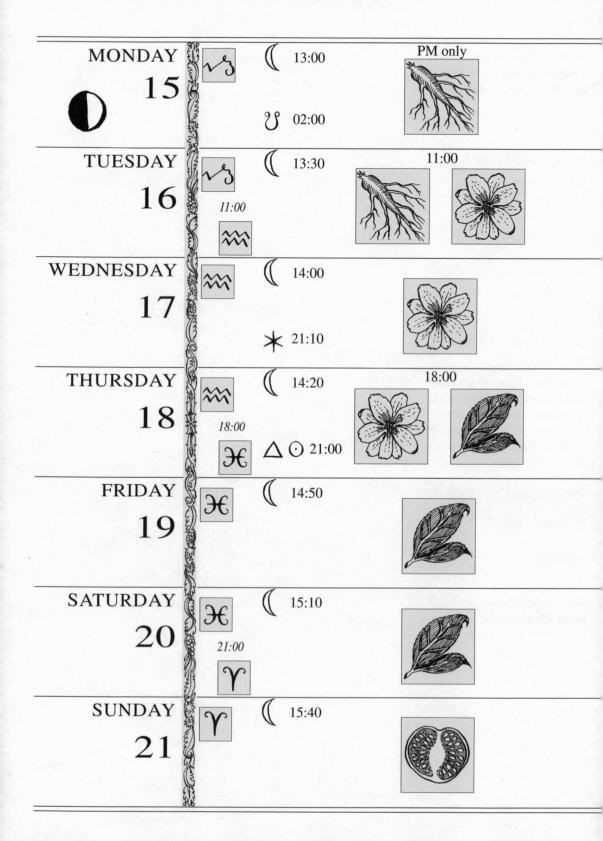

MONDAY 15

♑ ☾ 13:00 PM only

☊ 02:00

TUESDAY 16

♑ ☾ 13:30 11:00

11:00

♒

WEDNESDAY 17

♒ ☾ 14:00

✳ 21:10

THURSDAY 18

♒ ☾ 14:20 18:00

18:00

♓ △ ☉ 21:00

FRIDAY 19

♓ ☾ 14:50

SATURDAY 20

♓ ☾ 15:10

21:00

♈

SUNDAY 21

♈ ☾ 15:40

NOVEMBER

The Moon crosses the dragon's tail (south node) in the early hours, hence the recommendation to work only in the afternoon.

MONDAY
15

The change in elements happens mid-morning.

TUESDAY
16

The Moon and Saturn are sextile (60°).

WEDNESDAY
17

The Moon and Sun form a trine aspect. The ruling signs change early in the evening.

THURSDAY
18

FRIDAY
19

There is progression from leaf plants (Water) to fruit- and seed-bearing plants (Fire) in the middle of the evening.

SATURDAY
20

SUNDAY
21

 Libra
Air

 Scorpio
Water

 Sagittarius
Fire

 Capricorn
Earth

 Aquarius
Air

 Pisces
Water

NOVEMBER

MONDAY 22

♈ ☽ 16:10
22:00
♉ ♂ 02:30

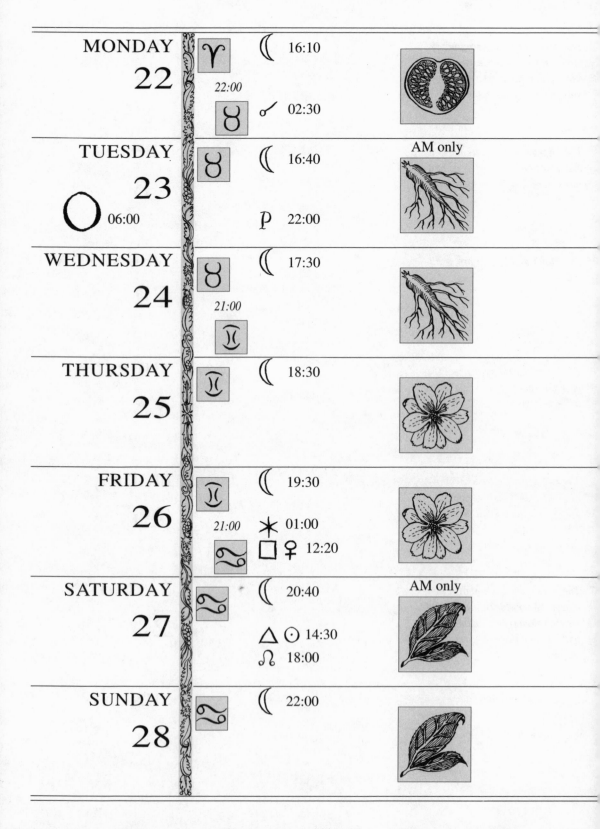

TUESDAY 23

♉ ☽ 16:40
○ 06:00
♇ 22:00

AM only

WEDNESDAY 24

♉ ☽ 17:30
21:00
♊

THURSDAY 25

♊ ☽ 18:30

FRIDAY 26

♊ ☽ 19:30
21:00
♋ ✳ 01:00
□ ♀ 12:20

SATURDAY 27

♋ ☽ 20:40
△ ☉ 14:30
♌ 18:00

AM only

SUNDAY 28

♋ ☽ 22:00

 Aries *Fire*   Taurus *Earth*   Gemini *Air*   Cancer *Water*   Leo *Fire*   Virgo *Earth*

NOVEMBER

The Moon forms a conjunction with Saturn. Elements change in the evening.

MONDAY
22

Full Moon early in the morning. The Moon's orbit reaches its perigee hence no planting before lunch.

TUESDAY
23

WEDNESDAY
24

THURSDAY
25

The Moon forms a square with Venus and is in a sextile aspect with Saturn. This is a good flower day – ending with a change of sign in the evening.

FRIDAY
26

The Moon crosses its north node at teatime, so no planting in the afternoon. It formed a trine aspect with the Sun nearer the middle of the day.

SATURDAY
27

SUNDAY
28

 Libra
Air

 Scorpio
Water

 Sagittarius
Fire

 Capricorn
Earth

 Aquarius
Air

 Pisces
Water

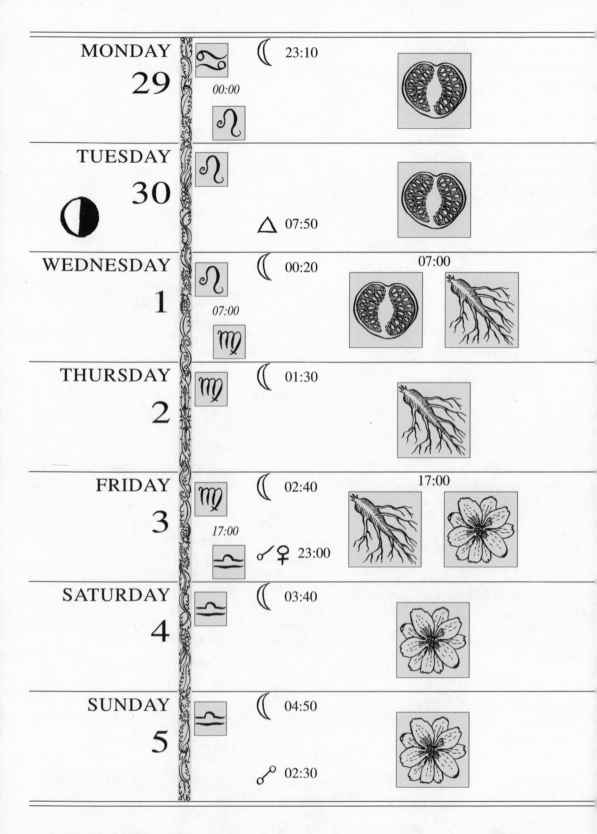

MONDAY 29

♋ 23:10
00:00
♌

TUESDAY 30

♌
△ 07:50

WEDNESDAY 1

♌ 00:20
07:00
♍
07:00

THURSDAY 2

♍ 01:30

FRIDAY 3

♍ 02:40
17:00
17:00
♎
⚲♀ 23:00

SATURDAY 4

♎ 03:40

SUNDAY 5

♎ 04:50
⚹ 02:30

♈ Aries *Fire*
♉ Taurus *Earth*
♊ Gemini *Air*
♋ Cancer *Water*
♌ Leo *Fire*
♍ Virgo *Earth*

NOVEMBER/DECEMBER

The change in ruling elements happens at the very turn of the day.

MONDAY
29

The Moon forms a trine aspect with Saturn early in the morning. This is a good day to work with trees, for instance pruning during the waning Moon.

TUESDAY
30

The change from fruit (Fire) to root (Earth) elements occurs at about breakfast time.

WEDNESDAY
1

THURSDAY
2

The change in elements happens at the end of the day. There is a conjunction (0°) between the Moon and Venus.

FRIDAY
3

SATURDAY
4

The Moon is in opposition (180°) to Saturn.

SUNDAY
5

 Libra *Air*   Scorpio *Water*   Sagittarius *Fire*   Capricorn *Earth*   Aquarius *Air*   Pisces *Water*

DECEMBER

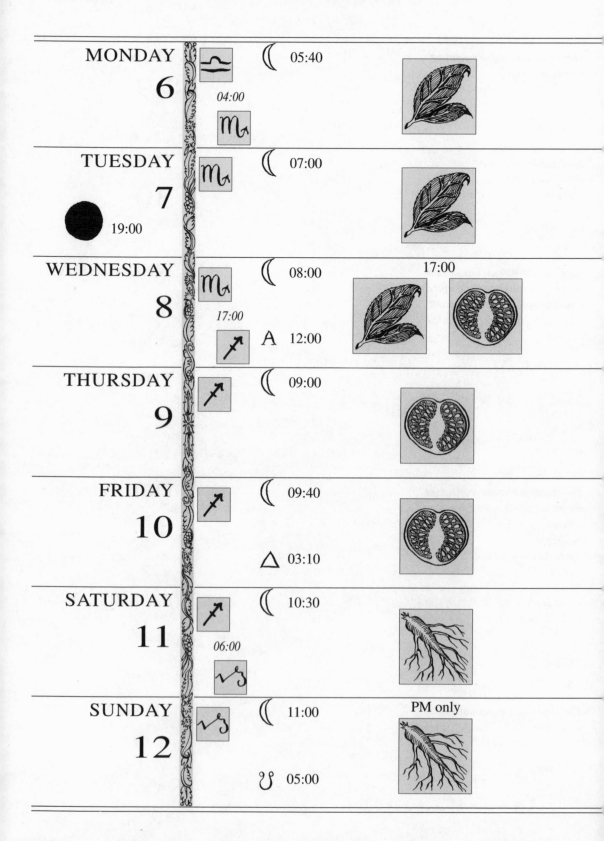

MONDAY 6
♎ 🌙 05:40
04:00
♏

TUESDAY 7
♏ 🌙 07:00
● 19:00

WEDNESDAY 8
♏ 🌙 08:00
17:00
17:00
♐ A 12:00

THURSDAY 9
♐ 🌙 09:00

FRIDAY 10
♐ 🌙 09:40
△ 03:10

SATURDAY 11
♐ 🌙 10:30
06:00
♑

SUNDAY 12
♑ 🌙 11:00
PM only
♈ 05:00

DECEMBER

There is a change in elements before work begins.	**MONDAY** **6**
New Moon.	**TUESDAY** **7**
At midday, the Moon reaches the apogee of its orbit of the earth, a time of imbalance. There is a shift from leaf to fruit/seed plants in the afternoon.	**WEDNESDAY** **8**
	THURSDAY **9**
The Moon and Saturn are trine in the middle of the night.	**FRIDAY** **10**
There is a change in elements in the early morning.	**SATURDAY** **11**
The Moon crosses its south node at the beginning of the day, work only in the afternoon.	**SUNDAY** **12**

 Libra
Air

 Scorpio
Water

 Sagittarius
Fire

 Capricorn
Earth

 Aquarius
Air

 Pisces
Water

DECEMBER

MONDAY 13 ♐ ☽ 11:40

18:00 ♒

18:00

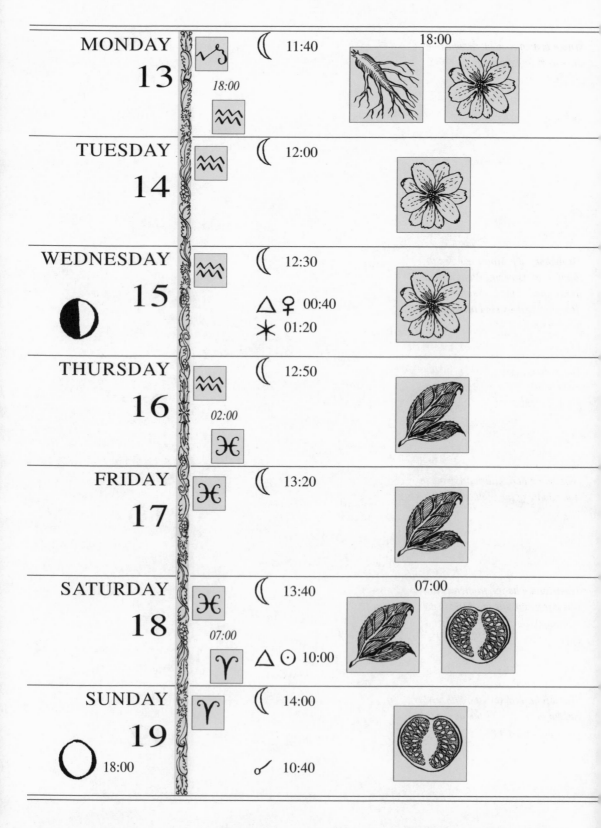

TUESDAY 14 ♒ ☽ 12:00

WEDNESDAY 15 ♒ ☽ 12:30

△ ♀ 00:40
⚹ 01:20

THURSDAY 16 ♒ ☽ 12:50

02:00 ♓

FRIDAY 17 ♓ ☽ 13:20

SATURDAY 18 ♓ ☽ 13:40

07:00 ♈

△ ☉ 10:00

07:00

SUNDAY 19 ♈ ☽ 14:00

○ 18:00

☌ 10:40

DECEMBER

The change in elements happens at the end of the afternoon.

MONDAY
13

TUESDAY
14

The Moon and Saturn are sextile (60°). The Moon and Venus form a trine aspect. This is another good flower day, particularly around the hours 12:00–14:00.

WEDNESDAY
15

The ruling signs change in the night hours, leaving the whole day for leaf plants.

THURSDAY
16

FRIDAY
17

There is progression from leaf (Water) to fruit/seed plants (Fire) in the morning. The Moon forms a trine aspect to the Sun.

SATURDAY
18

The Moon is in conjunction with Saturn.

SUNDAY
19

 Libra *Air*

 Scorpio *Water*

 Sagittarius *Fire*

 Capricorn *Earth*

 Aquarius *Air*

 Pisces *Water*

DECEMBER

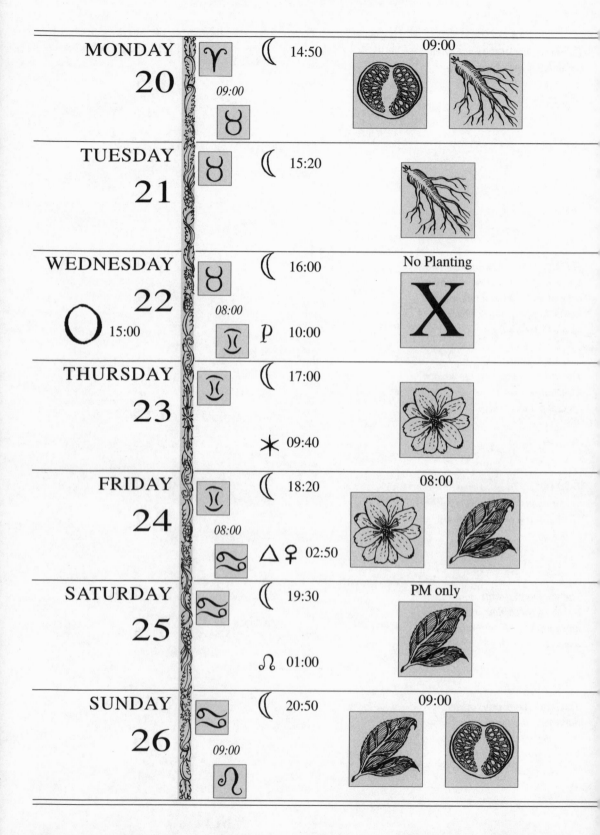

| MONDAY 20 | ♈ | ☾ 14:50 | 09:00 |
| | *09:00* ♉ | | |

| TUESDAY 21 | ♉ | ☾ 15:20 | |

| WEDNESDAY 22 ○ 15:00 | ♉ | ☾ 16:00 | No Planting **X** |
| | *08:00* ♊ ℞ 10:00 | | |

| THURSDAY 23 | ♊ | ☾ 17:00 ✳ 09:40 | |

| FRIDAY 24 | ♊ | ☾ 18:20 | 08:00 |
| | *08:00* ♋ △ ♀ 02:50 | | |

| SATURDAY 25 | ♋ | ☾ 19:30 ♌ 01:00 | PM only |

| SUNDAY 26 | ♋ | ☾ 20:50 | 09:00 |
| | *09:00* ♌ | | |

DECEMBER

There is a shift of elements at the beginning of the working day.

MONDAY

20

TUESDAY

21

Full Moon in the afternoon. The Moon reaches its perigee, a time of imbalance, hence no planting.

WEDNESDAY

22

The Moon forms a sextile aspect with Saturn.

THURSDAY

23

There is a progression from flower to leaf plants in the morning. The Moon forms a trine with Venus.

FRIDAY

24

The Moon crosses its north node at one o'clock in the morning, so no planting until the afternoon.

SATURDAY

25

As with all the changes of elements this week, the move from leaf to fruit/seed plants happens at the beginning of working hours.

SUNDAY

26

 Libra
Air

 Scorpio
Water

 Sagittarius
Fire

 Capricorn
Earth

 Aquarius
Air

 Pisces
Water

DECEMBER

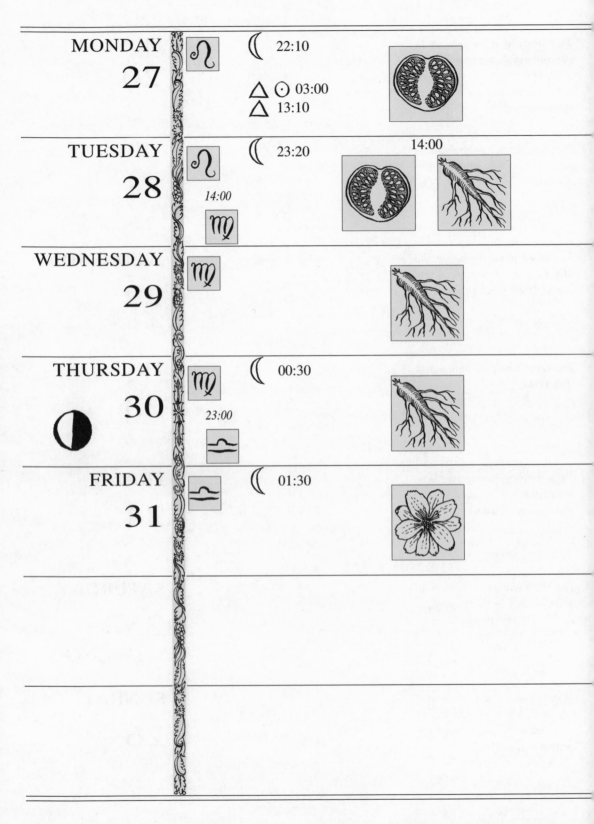

MONDAY 27
♌ ☽ 22:10
△ ☉ 03:00
△ 13:10

TUESDAY 28
♌ ☽ 23:20
14:00
♍

WEDNESDAY 29
♍

THURSDAY 30
♍ ☽ 00:30
23:00
≏

FRIDAY 31
≏ ☽ 01:30

DECEMBER

The Moon forms a trine aspect with the Sun early in the morning. Twelve hours later, it is with Saturn. Perhaps a good day to think of digging over the vegetable plot.

MONDAY

27

The change in ruling elements happens at the beginning of the afternoon.

TUESDAY

28

WEDNESDAY

29

The change from fruit (Fire) to root (Earth) elements occurs at nearly midnight, leaving the whole of the next day to devote to flowering plants.

THURSDAY

30

FRIDAY

31

 Libra
Air

 Scorpio
Water

 Sagittarius
Fire

 Capricorn
Earth

 Aquarius
Air

 Pisces
Water

NOTES

NOTES

NOTES

NOTES

NOTES

NOTES